A Farm Life

Observations from Fields and Forests

Daryln Brewer Hoffstot

STACKPOLE BOOKS

Essex, Connecticut
Blue Ridge Summit, Pennsylvania

STACKPOLE BOOKS

An imprint of Globe Pequot, the trade division of
The Rowman & Littlefield Publishing Group, Inc.
4501 Forbes Blvd., Ste. 200
Lanham, MD 20706
www.rowman.com

Distributed by NATIONAL BOOK NETWORK

"Elegy to a Sugar Maple" originally appeared as "Giving Thanks for a Beloved Sugar Maple"
© 2022 The New York Times Company.

"Marcellus Shale Seismic Testing" originally appeared as "Invasion of the Marcellus Men"
© 2011 *Pittsburgh Post-Gazette*, all rights reserved. Reprinted with permission.

"Quarantine on the Farm" originally appeared as "On a Pennsylvania Farm, 'Nature is Not Just
Carrying On'" © 2020 The New York Times Company.

A version of "Sharing a Small Patch of Earth" originally appeared in the Ideas section of
the *Boston Globe*.

All other essays first appeared in *Pittsburgh Quarterly*.

Illustrations from Getty Creative, except illustration of a sleeping porch on p. 96
courtesy of Ellis Schmidlapp.

Cover design by Mila Ratto

British Library Cataloguing in Publication Information available

Library of Congress Cataloging-in-Publication Data available

ISBN 978-0-8117-7245-7 (cloth)
ISBN 978-0-8117-7246-4 (electronic)

To my husband, son, and daughter,
the greatest joys of living on this farm.

"The world and our life in it are conditional gifts.
We have the world to live in
and the use of it to live from
on the condition that we will take good care of it.
And to take good care of it
we have to know it
and we have to know how to take care of it.
And to know it
and to be willing to take care of it,
we have to love it."

—WENDELL BERRY

CONTENTS

Acknowledgments

With thanks to Douglas Heuck for letting me try my hand at writing "A Farm Life" for *Pittsburgh Quarterly* and to Douglas Alteen for publishing my essays in the *New York Times*.

To John Wenzel, who always answered my scientific questions with kindness and passion and to all the entomologists, biologists, ornithologists, and other experts who taught me so much.

Thanks to Susan Cheever and Maxwell King for their advice and friendship.

Gratitude and love to Mila Ratto for her beautiful cover design and to Amber Caron, a superb writer and editor and a dear friend, whose enthusiasm propelled this book forward.

> *"A friend may well be reckoned the masterpiece of nature."*
> —Ralph Waldo Emerson

INTRODUCTION

I MOVED TO OUR WESTERN PENNSYLVANIA FARM FROM NEW YORK CITY thirty-five years ago. I was recently married, wanted to live in an old farmhouse, and hoped to raise our not-yet-conceived children in a place where they could catch crayfish in a stream and climb hay bales in a barn. I couldn't wait to have a garden and a compost heap. I imagined walking in deep snow, cutting our Christmas tree, and hauling it home on a sled. I wanted us to be surrounded by animals.

The literary organization I worked for allowed me to work remotely for a while—way before a pandemic hit and such became common practice—and as I spent more time on the farm and less in the city, I set out to teach myself about the natural world. My husband and I had already become interested in birds—we liked birding in Central Park and when traveling—but I had grown up in the suburbs and worked in cities, so I had a lot to learn. He's collected, over many years, an impressive array of birding books from around the world, and now those—along with field guides on mushrooms, herbs, insects, butterflies, wildflowers, edible plants, stars, mosses, reptiles, animal tracks, minerals, shrubs, and trees—overflow from the bookshelf at the foot of our front hall stairs. Despite the ease of the Internet, I refer to them regularly. *Caterpillars of Eastern North America* is my most recent addition, purchased after I read how crucial caterpillars are to a bird's diet. I still have a lot to learn.

In time, we were lucky enough to have a son and then a daughter, and I tried in my own small way to help them appreciate the wonder of it all. We hiked, rode horses, and snowshoed in the woods, across fields, along streams, through pine forests and swamps—two dogs, sometimes three, always in tow. The children chased fireflies, picked wild blackberries, built forts in the woods. I began foraging, and one of my fondest memories is a warm, spring day when my thirteen-year-old daughter and I were horseback riding. Trotting on a field's edge, she looked down to see a huge, golden morel. We rode back to the barn, untacked the horses, put them in the field, and returned to that spot, where we found thirty-three gigantic morels, the best stash ever.

Whenever I was in the woods, no matter what the activity, I thought of poet Mary Oliver, who urged her readers to observe nature, be astonished by it, and to tell the world. Her words became my mantra. I observed even more closely, had no shortage of astonishment, and when I found myself wanting to tell about it, I proposed a column to *Pittsburgh Quarterly* called "A Farm Life," which has run for six years.

I knew, of course, that we lived in a beautiful valley nestled between two ridges of the Allegheny Mountains, with a barn and a pond and an old spring house that doubles as a chicken coop, but it was only in the writing about the plants and animals on our farm that I came to understand what a special property it is. Our mail carrier told me she once left our property with two large paper bags full of morels. Our furnace repairman used to sneak into the forest with his uncle to hunt ginseng. People from miles away find their way into the woods to dig ramps. Perhaps that's because the previous owner kept the place intact for forty years, as we have for nearly as long, allowing nature to do as it wishes. As Aldo Leopold said, "The oldest task in human history: to live on a piece of land without spoiling it." We have tried to be good stewards.

Writing about life on the farm suited me. I loved staying home and living in blue jeans. I didn't miss the city much—except my friends—and I relished the slower pace. I came to appreciate the art of observation, a trait I fear, with our busy lives and noses stuck in cell phones, is becoming extinct. And it's not just city children—many children who live here don't know the flora and the fauna in their own backyards. John Wenzel, then director of nearby Powdermill Nature Reserve, gave me perhaps the greatest compliment when, after reading my *New York Times* article, "On a Pennsylvania Farm, 'Nature Is Not Just Carrying On,'" he wrote to say that I was a person who has the insight to KNOW the land on which she lives. (CAPS his.) There were times in my life when I wanted to be fluent in French or write a perfect short story, but when John wrote those words to me, I was immensely satisfied simply to begin to know the land on which I live.

The art of observation is not the only thing headed toward extinction. My first column, in the spring of 2017, described the loss of thousands of ash trees on our farm. We heard limbs crack and watched mighty trunks succumb to the invasive emerald ash borer, which has killed hundreds of millions of trees across North America. In a short period of time, the brilliant green beetle changed the nature of the forest as we knew it, and it will not be the same again, at least in my lifetime. In another column, I found joy watching feral honeybees set up housekeeping in a hole in a walnut tree by our barn—particularly moved, I think, because I knew we'd lost 40 percent of the honeybees in this country. One of my favorite columns described the lives of chimney swifts, fascinating birds that spend all day airborne, whose numbers have fallen by 72 percent and which we've allowed to nest in our nineteenth-century chimney.

Observing and writing about these and other subjects has made me understand better the terrible threat of climate change and has convinced me that many people won't take climate change seriously until they see, with their own eyes and in their own backyards, the climate's effect on bees, trees, bugs, bats, streams, plants, birds, amphibians, and the land. I consider part of my job writing this column to look at those truths. We take common plants and animals for granted now, but who knows how long bumblebees, chipmunks, black rat snakes, and pileated woodpeckers will occupy my backyard? Or, for that matter, be here at all? Great auks roamed the earth once too . . .

In a column I wrote on stinging nettles, Adam Haritan, a local forager and educator, said, "I don't think we give the land we live on enough credit. We always want to go to exotic places." At the beginning of the pandemic, I had some hope that staying home might make us all more aware of the land on which we live, maybe even think about better protecting the plants and animals among us. But so far, I am not seeing the change for which I'd hoped. We have only a short time on this planet to try to make it better, and from my local perspective, we have a lot of work to do.

TREES, PLANTS, AND FUNGI

The Ash Tree

ASH TREES ARE FALLING ALL OVER OUR FARM—IN THE WOODS, ON THE driveway, by our front door. We walk under these trees, ride horses by them, mow the lawn around their trunks. Dogs doze underneath. I have sat on our porch and watched limbs crash to the ground, grateful I was not planting bulbs in the soil below. I consider avoiding the woods altogether, but I cannot do that; the woods are my solace. Still, when I do walk there, I look up more than usual. Saddest, perhaps, is the ash by our front door, fifty feet high, with a crown like a martini glass. That tree was here long before we were—when we looked at the property in 1988, brought our son home from the hospital in 1990 and our daughter in 1994—standing sentry over this house, and our lives.

Ash trees aren't just dying in Pennsylvania. They're dying all over the Northeast, and beyond. "Texas just got on board," said Brian Crooks, a forester with the Western Pennsylvania Conservancy. A month later, Nebraska was hit, then Delaware, and as of this writing, thirty-five states and five Canadian provinces have been infested with the emerald ash borer (EAB).

The half-inch long, shiny green beetle arrived from Asia in wood packing material, probably in cargo ships, or perhaps by airplane, and was first detected in Detroit in 2002, before which the beetle had never been seen in North America. But Dr. Deborah McCullough, a professor of forest entomology at Michigan State University and an EAB expert, said a tree-ring study subsequently revealed that the beetle had been in Michigan at least ten years before that. This crafty little insect spread across state lines by hitching rides in timber, firewood, and nursery trees—and within a few years an infestation was born. (There is now a quarantine for moving ash across most state borders in affected states.)

The emerald ash borer was first detected in Pennsylvania in Cranberry Township in 2007 and detected here in Westmoreland County in 2009. Now, nearly all the ash trees at our farm look like ghostly skeletons against an otherwise green background.

The emerald ash borer attacks predominately ash trees, of which there are 305 million in Pennsylvania. We have five native species, the most common being green, white, and black. McCullough said green and black are the "preferred host. They get clobbered." But in the field in western Pennsylvania, Crooks said he sees the destruction mostly of white ash.

The top third of our sentry ash began to die back first, normal for trees attacked by the insect. Adult beetles feed on the leaves in springtime, causing no damage, but then the females lay eggs, which hatch, and the larvae tunnels inside the tree, forming S-shaped tunnels, where they feed on the inner bark. That's where the damage occurs, cutting off the tree's food and water. "Basically, the tree starves to death," McCullough said. The following spring, adult beetles reemerge, and the cycle begins again.

The beetles are difficult to see in the wild, but not so the beetle's one-eighth-inch D-shaped exit holes in the tree's bark, nor the holes left by woodpeckers, which prey on the ash borer larvae. I've also seen "bark flaking," where the bark falls off, leaving the tree bare. Crooks said he sees devastation everywhere in Pennsylvania—in the city, on the turnpike, and in suburban yards, where the ash has been a popular tree with landowners "because of its big-tunnel shade effect." And as any baseball fan knows, losing white ash trees is bad for the industry, which has traditionally used the

3

wood to manufacture bats. "The emerald ash borer is the most destructive and costly forest insect to invade North America," McCullough said.

We have begun to cut our ash trees down—starting with the those that pose a danger around the house, about twenty so far—and that's only the beginning. Felling trees is costly and causes a colossal mess. Chemical treatments exist, which involve drilling into the trunk and injecting insecticide, which McCullough said has improved since 2002, but trees must be treated before they are severely injured. "If half the canopy is alive, it's worth using," she said.

Crooks suggested contacting a board-certified arborist to decide what to do with dying ash trees. "Anyone can walk out there with a bucket truck and say they're an arborist, but they're not going to give advice about how to replace trees." When replacing ash, Crooks advised planting different varieties. "Diversity is your friend," he said, suggesting swamp white oak, American sycamore, London planetree, hackberry, and disease-resistant elm cultivars like 'Accolade,' 'Emerald Sunshine,' and 'Morton Glossy.'

In his book *The Hidden Life of Trees*, German forester Peter Wohlleben wrote that trees transmit electrical signals between themselves to share news about insects, drought, and other dangers via fungal networks at their root tips "like fiber-optic Internet cables," which some call "the wood wide web." Trees may communicate also by sound waves, he wrote. Beech, spruce, and oak may register pain when a creature nibbles on them.

Reading that, I thought I would never look at trees the same way again. What, I wondered, might our ash trees might be saying to each other about the emerald ash borer?

My husband and I mourn the loss of our ash trees, and it is sobering to think that neither of us will be around to see so many ash trees this size again. But then I read Diana Beresford-Kroeger's book *To Speak for the Trees*, in which she wrote of a giant eastern white cedar which had been felled, leaving only the stump. "The stump before me wasn't living, not in the same way the tree it belonged to had been, but it *was* alive. Those big boles still take in water; they change shape; there is a form of life still present in them."

Ash trees alive, but in a different form? I will sit gingerly on a stump and contemplate this.

Elder

IN *HARRY POTTER & THE DEATHLY HOLLOWS*, THE MOST POWERFUL WAND IN
the world is made from the elder tree.

Who knew that the straggly shrub perched at the edge of our pond held
such powers? That its tiny, white, star-shaped flowers have long been used in
Europe for syrup and cordials, its dark purple berries for jelly, pies, and reme-
dies? Nor would I have predicted, as I write this sheltered at home during the
beginning of the coronavirus pandemic, that people would horde elderberry to
ward off Covid-19.

In the British Isles, European elder (*Sambucus nigra*) is "more like a tree,"
said Mason Heberling, assistant curator of botany at Pittsburgh's Carnegie
Museum of Natural History, and, when coppiced or pollarded, is often part
of England's hedgerows. Years ago, my friends in Ireland introduced me to
their homemade elderflower syrup mixed with sparkling water, which I loved,
but it was years before I realized that the more shrub-like American elder
(*Sambucus canadensis*) is indigenous to Pennsylvania and grows wild on our
Westmoreland County farm. When I finally figured that out, I attempted to
make my own syrup, failing miserably.

The good news for foragers like me is that elder can be found throughout our country "from the Atlantic to the Rockies, the Gulf of Mexico to
Quebec," said Patrick Byers, who's studying elder and human health at the
University of Missouri. "It has an amazing range." Greeks and Romans
used elder, he said, as well as Europeans, Asians, and Native Americans,
but elder products in the U.S. are relatively new. Only recently has elder
shown up in craft cocktails, wines, jellies, soft drinks, tea, juice, concentrate,
syrup, and more.

In 1997, Byer's state of Missouri had no cultivation of elder; now they have
over three hundred acres, where research is underway to examine the link
between elderberry, viruses, and brain health. Initially they studied only the
fruit but are currently looking at the flowers too. "There's great interest now in
the elderberry and its medicinal value," he said.

According to herbalists, elder's healing properties are extensive—as a diuretic, laxative, anti-inflammatory, to expel mucus, and to treat gynecological problems, gout, burns, headaches, eczema, coughs, ringworm, and sore throats. Native Americans considered it a blood purifier and a cure for dropsy, liver troubles, and a host of other ailments. Carrying a knotted elder twig in your pocket may ward off rheumatism. In 400 BCE, Hippocrates is said to have called the shrub a medicine chest.

"The tree was once part of every medicinal garden, monastery garden, and farmyard," wrote Ria Loohuizen in her book *The Elder*. "People planted it wherever they settled, in order to have its beneficial products always at hand." But in this country, we've been slow to catch on. As Euell Gibbons wrote in *Stalking the Wild Asparagus*, "elderberry is one of the most abundant, most useful, most healthful and yet most neglected of our native wild fruits."

Some say the branches, leaves, seeds, and roots contain a form of cyanide and should not be eaten raw or in excess. In 1983, twenty-five members of a California religious community were sickened by drinking juice made of uncooked berries, leaves, and branches of *Sambucus mexicana*. "We attempted to answer the cyanide concern in our research program," Byers said. His studies showed that while cyanide precursors were present in the elderberry products they tested, levels were "lower in fact than the apple juice samples."

Still, be prudent when eating in the wild. Byers advised heating or fermenting fruits and flowers and eliminating stems and leaves. "Some people are very sensitive to cyanide and cyanide precursors," he said.

American elder, once classified as a honeysuckle but now in the viburnum family, grows four to fifteen feet, with white flower clusters called corymbs that are three to ten inches in diameter. The shrub requires relatively high light so is usually seen on the wood's edge. Nine species exist worldwide, on every continent except Antarctica, and once identified, it's easy to spot. I've seen elder blooming on the side streets in Bogota, Colombia, on Route 95 in south Florida, and on the Pennsylvania turnpike.

"The wood is distinctive because it has a hollow stem," Heberling said, with a whitish pith easily removed. For that reason, elder stems have been made into peashooters, flutes, whistles, maple syrup spouts, popguns, and bellows. Mature wood is hard, used for carving and whittling, and made into pegs, spindles, and combs.

Myths surrounding the tree abound. The Druids viewed elder as a holy tree, believing that those who sat under it on midsummer's eve might see the Fairy King and Queen. Sleeping beneath a blooming elder protected against snakes and mosquitos, and elder defended cattle against lightning. When elder crosses placed on coffins sprouted, that meant the spirit had departed. The elder mother—called Lady Ellhorn in Britain and Hylde Moer in Danish—was believed to live inside the tree. She insisted that people obtain permission—hands folded and on bended knee—to cut branches. As I am not one to get on the bad side of an old superstition, you can bet I was on bended knee when I cut a stem to look at its pithy channel.

Should you wish to plant your own, "elder is one of the most rewarding plants in terms of propagation," Byers said. Hardwood cuttings can be potted in a growing medium or planted directly into soil. Softwood cuttings, root cuttings, and planting seeds are other ways to grow the plant. According to Penn State, elder likes well-drained soil with a pH between 5.5 and 6.5 and cultivation should be shallow. Plants come into full production after three to four years.

When foraging for elderberries "make sure you're harvesting elderberry, first of all," Byers said, explaining that elder can be confused with poke-berry and greenbrier. One of the beauties of elder is that there are two harvests—flowers and berries—but leave enough flowers so the berries will come on, and some berries for birds and bears, who depend on the shrub for food. Flower blossoms should be open and dry. "The best aroma is when all the florets are open," Byers said. Never pick bruised or damaged flowers, remove as much of the stem as possible, and don't store flowers in plastic.

Flowers should be used as soon as possible or dried for later use. Make sure berries are ripe.

The good news is that elder is not threatened or endangered, Heberling said. "It is prolific, with lots of seeds." However, like many other native species, elder is becoming less common in North American forests due to hungry deer, he said. And since some homeowners consider the scrawny-looking shrub a weed, they chop it down. Byers doesn't worry about climate change, calling elder "an adaptable and resilient plant."

I believe my initial failure at making elderflower syrup was boiling the water, which some recipes call for, but my Irish friends do not. In her book, Loohuizen claimed boiling leads to a noticeable loss of flavor and aroma, which was the case with my syrup. Most recipes call for a combination of elderflower, sugar, lemon, and sometimes citric acid. Flowers dipped in batter, fried, and topped with icing sugar is another elderflower favorite, though I haven't tried it yet.

Linda Sinemus, who sold produce at the Ligonier Farmer's Market for eighteen years, has made elderberry jelly from her grandmother's favorite recipe since she was a young girl. She boils elderberries in a steamer, extracts the juice, and combines it with sugar and pectin. "My son doesn't make peanut butter and jelly sandwiches with anything but elderberry jelly," she said.

Her father used to drive the tractor to a stand of elder on the farm, put Sinemus on a high lift, and raise her up to fetch the berries, one of her fondest memories. "I'd dive into the middle of the bushes," she said, snip the flowers and put them in a basket, and her father would lower her down. Trees on her Latrobe farm bloom in late May to early June and berries ripen from mid-July to mid-August. But you've got to beat the birds. "They'll clean the entire bush," she said.

"Elder grew everywhere when we were younger," Sinemus said, "but a lot of spraying along the roadways has killed off most of the shrubs." That is lamentable, she said, as people depended on elder for food, especially during the Depression.

Harvesting food in your own backyard seems like a pretty good idea to me during a global pandemic. Just remember to fold your hands and get down on bended knee.

Elegy to a Sugar Maple

STANDING UNDER THE OLD SUGAR MAPLE, I WANT TO SING A HYMN. KNEEL down and pray. Its tall branches tower above me like flying buttresses, its wide canopy is a sanctuary. It is my favorite tree on the farm.

I measure its girth: 13½ feet in circumference. Not as large as the maple that was felled in New Hampshire in 2021. That tree was a national champion: 19 feet in circumference, 101 feet tall, with a canopy that stretched 100 feet. Our maple, no record holder, is smaller—about 90 feet tall with a 70-foot canopy—but still of a size one doesn't see every day. I can stand underneath the tree in the rain and barely get wet. My husband and I guess the tree is about the age of our old log house, circa 1860, but we're not sure—young perhaps for maples, which can live two or three hundred years. I don't know if it ever brought forth its sweet syrup as other maples have in this valley, but a friend who grew up here and has tapped sugar maples for fifty years, says he's never seen a bigger *Acer saccharum*.

The maple lives at the bottom of a hill where our children used to sled ride in winter and jump into colorful leaf piles in autumn. Sometime long before we arrived at our western Pennsylvania farm thirty-four years ago, the tree split into four. I remember our son climbing into the hollow that formed, where ferns now grow. We hung maple samaras—helicopters—on our noses. The maple's gnarly roots protrude out of the ground like those you'd see illustrated in *Alice in Wonderland*.

The old sugar maple sits next to the spring and the spring house—which we turned into a chicken coop—good and bad, I've observed, for while the maple's maze of branches offers the chickens some protection, it also offers multiple perches for owls and hawks to plan attacks. Fox, racoon, fisher, and opossum circle the tree furtively, scouting out their next meal. Snakes and mice do too. Squirrels, which presumably call the maple home, race to and fro, gathering nuts for their winter larder. Bird life fills the tree. In spring, the tree erupts with a dawn chorus of migrating birds and in summer the tiny Carolina wren belts out its glorious song. After the birds have

flown south, I look up to see a multitude of nests. One, very high up,
might be that of a Baltimore
oriole, which I love because
of the way their nests hang
like sporrans.

Today when I collect
eggs though, I worry a
branch will hit me on the
head. I'm concerned for
the chickens too, wise
as they are to impending
danger. I have heard them
squawk and seen them race
away from the cracking branches
before they tumble.

The old maple is dying.

It faded slowly at first, but last
summer it began to go fast, its lichen-covered
limbs snapping and falling to the ground, the gray bark covered with dark
green moss. It has far fewer leaves. A crack runs up the middle. More plants
grow in the tree's crevices: purple blackberry canes, spiky grasses, and red-
tinged euonymus. For the first time, I see three woodpecker holes, so beautifully aligned they look like Orion's belt.

I do not know why the tree is dying so I do some research. Maples have
many diseases, such as anthracnose, verticillium wilt, and powdery mildew,
but I am still confused, so I call Brian Crooks, a forester with the Western
Pennsylvania Conservancy. The giveaway, he says, are the small honey-colored
button mushrooms at the tree's base, which indicate the maple has a fungus—
Armillaria root rot.

The *Armillaria* fungus affects many hardwoods and conifers, especially
maples, oaks, and elms. Black, stringy rhizomorphs grow through the soil
into the roots and trunk of the tree and attack the wood. If I remove the
bark, I might see bright, white mycelial fans. But none of that is visible—yet.
I learn that the *Armillaria* fungus is the world's largest known organism—
bigger than the 200-ton blue whale—a patch of which was discovered in
Oregon in 1998 covering 2,384 acres. I don't know how large ours is, but I
do worry about it encroaching on a nearby tree—a large red oak—a favorite
of my husband's.

I wonder if the maple doesn't like our new western Pennsylvania weather: the extreme heat, the drought, then the microbursts of rain and wind and the flash floods. When our floods come now, the water runs down the hill so fast that the maple sits in the middle of a pond, a stream running through it. I do know from sugaring with my friend and his eighty-nine-year-old uncle that changing climatic conditions are making sugaring more difficult. For the sap to run in February or March, the days must be warm and the nights cold and the timing is less predictable now. But I am not a scientist, so I ask Crooks.

He tells me that while *Armillaria* fungus is nothing new, western Pennsylvania is becoming more favorable for fungal development. Sudden periods of wet and then dry increase stress on the tree and allow fungi to more easily infiltrate a tree's root system. Individual trees and entire forests are becoming less resilient against pests and disease due to climate change.

For our old maple, the *Armillaria* fungus is a death knell. There is no way for the tree to recover. "Once it colonizes the root system and displays visible mushrooms, the fungus is well progressed within the tree," Crooks says. "Sorry to have to share bad news."

"Standing people" is what the Cherokee called trees.

I feel as if I am losing a member of the family.

Now when I close the chicken coop at night, I stand at the altar and

give a eulogy. I say how grateful I am to have spent a third of a century under its gaze. I thank the tree for its contribution to this farm—for standing by my family in good times and bad. I whisper a prayer for whatever is the afterlife of trees, and hum a favorite hymn, *Ein feste Burg*, singing a sad goodbye to what was, indeed, a mighty fortress.

Making Maple Syrup

I STUCK A SPOON IN THE FINISHING PAN AND TASTED THE SAP—SWEET, BUT too thin, said my friend teaching me how to make maple syrup. At eighty-nine, he's been sugaring on his family farm for years, and now he's instructing his grandnephews, the fourth generation, who kindly allowed me to tag along.

It wasn't going well. Warm temperatures in late winter and early spring challenged syrup makers across the southwestern part of our state. The nights got too warm, the sap slowed, and they worried the end product wouldn't taste good.

Temperature is just one of many factors that can affect syrup. The type of tree matters, the soil it's planted in, and when it's tapped. Wind can slow the dripping of the sap, and if the trees begin to bud, the liquid becomes what's called "buddy syrup" and is ruined.

The process is labor intensive. The sugar camp needs to be tidied, firewood chopped, and materials organized: buckets, lids, spiles, thermometers, filters, and jugs. It's a twenty-four-hour-a-day job because sap, a colorless liquid resembling water with a 2-percent sugar content, must be cooked down to 66 percent sugar, and it takes forty-three gallons of sap to make one gallon of syrup. Sometimes my friend sleeps overnight at the camp, stoking the fire and taking the temperature of the liquid—219 degrees, or seven degrees above water's boiling point, is ideal. The liquid mustn't boil over or burn. "If you don't keep your eye on it, *something* happens," he said.

Pennsylvania's sugaring season typically takes place in February and March and lasts six weeks, but that's changing. Dr. Timothy Perkins, director of the Proctor Maple Research Center at the University of Vermont, believes climate change has shifted the season to earlier in the year, causing "uncertainty for producers," he said. Last year's weather was even weirder. "Backward," my friend said, cold in fall when it should have been warm, and warm in winter when it should have been cold. In a half century, he couldn't remember a worse sugaring year.

Ideal sugaring weather is when nights are below freezing and days are in the forties. Warming temperatures create pressure within the tree, which forces sap—or starch stored in the wood—to be released. The aptly named sugar maple (*Acer sacchurum*) is the most commonly tapped tree because of its high sugar content. A twelve-inch diameter tree, about forty years old, generally gets one tap. Larger trees might get two, three at the most.

Legends abound as to how maple syrup was discovered. One says an Iroquois chief threw a tomahawk into a tree at night, the weather warmed, and the next day his wife used sap instead of water to cook venison, sweetening the dish. Dr. Perkins said Native Americans probably learned from watching birds and animals, particularly squirrels. In early spring on windy, sunny days, squirrels nip shallow grooves into maple branches, wait for the sap to dry into sugar granules, and eat it. Native Americans likely taught English and French settlers—and an industry was born.

Canada produces the most syrup in the world, 12.2 million gallons valued at $487 million, of which Quebec accounts for 92 percent. The U.S. produces about 4.2 million gallons valued at $147 million, with Vermont the largest producer of a half a million gallons. Pennsylvania ranks from fifth to seventh according to Penn State, producing 60,000 gallons per year, valued at $1.9 million. Nearby Somerset County is our state's biggest producer.

Modern day commercial operations involve using vacuums attached to plastic tubing that runs from trees to sugar camp, and using reverse osmosis, invented in the 1970s, which removes water from the sap before boiling. The latter changes syrup's taste, my friend claimed, but Dr. Perkins said his center has conducted studies comparing what he termed "techno syrup" to syrup made by more traditional methods, and people can't tell the difference.

We made our syrup in a more old-fashioned way, going out into the sugarbush on a perfect day—forty-one degrees and sunny—drilling holes, plugging them with spiles, and hanging galvanized tin buckets. We collected the sap by hand. I tapped a few of our trees too and added the sap to the lot. Granted, we transported the sap to the sugar camp via an all-terrain vehicle— alas, we had no horse-drawn sleigh—but it still felt as if we were performing a task few do anymore. We poured the sap into a holding tank, then through a filtration system of wool felt to remove any impurities, into a wood-fired evaporator, and finally a finishing pan.

The USDA has three Grade A syrup classifications: light amber, medium amber, and dark amber, and one Grade B, which is darker, with a stronger maple flavor. I prefer early syrup, generally lighter in color with a milder taste, but it's difficult to come by, so I put whatever grade syrup I can get into my green tea each morning.

Some of our syrup was bottled, but in the end, all of it had to be thrown away. It tasted terrible. Dr. Perkins asked me what went wrong, but I had no idea, so I asked him the same question. Two possible explanations were that we didn't boil the sap soon enough—sap must be boiled right away or it can ferment. Or that we boiled some sap and later added more to the same batch, which can make syrup "ropey or stringy," he said. "One of the hardest parts of this job is trying to diagnose the failures."

I doubt we'll ever know for sure, but I do know my friend and his family will be back at it again next year, welcoming company in the sugar camp to help pass the hours. People do stop by and say hello, bring snacks, and offer assistance, but nothing like the old days when they helped a lot more. People are too busy now, my friend said, too plugged-in to step back in time. But you'll find me there in February, undistracted, hoping for sweeter results.

Ginseng

I AM GRATEFUL FOR THE LOCALS WHO'VE TAUGHT ME SO MUCH ABOUT RURAL life. Our mail carrier showed me morels, our babysitter taught me about "onion snow," and last fall, Gary, our furnace expert, took me ginseng hunting—on our farm.

Gary is in his forties now, but he first came to our woods before we lived here to hunt ginseng as a boy with his uncle. "In the eighties, when the guys were out of work, they were all in these woods hunting ginseng," he said. Sometimes even the employed called off work because selling ginseng was more lucrative than a paycheck. "Nowadays, you still have to go to work," Gary said, wistfully.

That's because American ginseng (*Panax quinquefolius*), once abundant in the Appalachians from Georgia to Quebec, has been overharvested. "Virtually anywhere there's ginseng it's been overhunted at some point in the past or present," said James B. McGraw, PhD, professor emeritus at West Virginia University. Still, Pennsylvania ranks in the top five to ten states supplying ginseng to Asian and American markets.

"We have some of the best, highest quality ginseng in the world growing in our woods," said Dr. Eric Burkhart, a ginseng expert at Penn State University. North Central Pennsylvania and the Laurel Highlands produce the biggest crop, and Fayette County, not far from our farm, is "the number one export county." Burkhart lamented that Pennsylvania has neither recognized nor promoted its ginseng resource.

Ginseng has been coveted in Asia for thousands of years and in the New World for centuries because many believe the plant to be a panacea for a variety of ills, including fatigue, fertility, memory, insomnia, inflammation, erectile dysfunction, and stress. The list is long and the results often unproven. Asians regard ginseng as a tonic (yang) from which they get energy, and the Americans as a relaxant (yin). I asked McGraw whether he believed the claims, and he said: "Many people will say, 'millions and millions of Asian users can't all be wrong.'" Testimonials abound, including this one from a ginseng hunter in

Foxfire 3: "I'll tell you one thing, you can be in the woods and take a stomachache or the old hungry colic, and you can just chew up some of the fine roots and swallow the juice of it and it won't be five or ten minutes your stomach'll be just as easy as you please."

Because of the plant's presumed powers, "very savvy" Asian buyers send trucks from New York City into the eastern U.S. mountains to purchase barrels of ginseng from local dealers, McGraw said. Yearly exports of sixty thousand to one hundred sixty thousand pounds of wild ginseng are shipped to Hong Kong, then on to China, Korea, and points beyond. Americans buy it too. "Well over $100 million a year on items that list ginseng as an ingredient," writes David A. Taylor in his book *Ginseng, the Divine Root*.

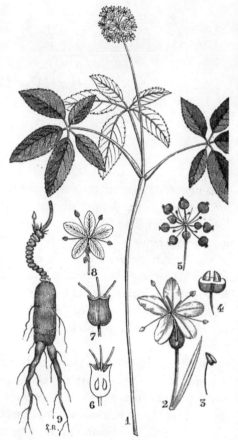

Ginseng is a slow-growing, long-lived perennial that Burkhart said can live one hundred years. Its taproot looks a bit like a human figure, which the Chinese call "human root." Asians prefer "truly wild" ginseng, the roots of which are "wrinkled, gnarly, and twisted," McGraw said. Asians pay the most for wild ginseng too—in Pennsylvania, an average of $700 per pound, dried. About 205 dried roots make a pound.

With its regional nicknames such as sang, seng, and shang, wild ginseng grows in our deciduous woods, in rich loamy soil, primarily on north- or east-facing slopes, and grows six to twelve inches high, though Burkhart has seen it "ankle to knee high." Its central stalk produces an umbel of greenish-white flowers in summer and a cluster of red berries in late summer or fall. From that stalk grow leaves, or "prongs"—ginseng vernacular—and each prong has one to five serrated leaflets. It takes five to ten years to reach the three-prong stage, which is when the plant starts to reproduce.

Wild simulated ginseng garners the next highest price and is grown by farmers in a forest setting, mimicking the wild. Burkhart believes Pennsylvanians should consider farming ginseng this way, both as a cash crop—demand is currently higher than supply—and to take pressure off the native plant. A third type, farmed ginseng, fetches the least amount of money. It is grown under artificial shade and is more susceptible to disease, often requiring fertilizers and fungicides. The biggest producers of farmed ginseng are in Wisconsin, Ontario, and British Columbia.

In thirty years, only one man has ever knocked on our door asking to hunt ginseng, but not long ago, in the early morning, my husband found an elderly man, inebriated, and two boys at our tractor shed, looking for ginseng. The season runs from September 1 to November 30.

During last year's season, Gary and his already-expert thirteen-year-old daughter, Emily, and I went out on a cool, September afternoon, when the sun's warmth felt delightful against the skin. Remnants of Hurricane Florence had just passed through, and the skies had cleared. Goldenrod and purple aster were in bloom, and puffballs and chicken-of-the-woods mushrooms were fruiting. I wiped spider webs from my face as we bushwhacked through the woods.

Gary led me to the area where he used to hunt. We've since built a woodshed nearby, but otherwise haven't altered the landscape. I scoured the forest floor, but I was not a natural "sang" hunter. I kept thinking I'd located one, but mistook ginseng for Virginia creeper, which vines throughout our woods. Other plants can fool you too: hickory seedlings, wild sarsaparilla—called fool's sang—and Ohio buckeye. Poison ivy can mimic young ginseng, and people have mistaken ginseng for marijuana, in the event that you see that growing in the woods . . .

"If you see red berries, that's a good sign," Gary said, as I kept trying—and failing—to find the elusive plant. He told me ginseng is easier to spot later in the season when it dies back and the foliage turns yellow. Another ginseng hunter in *Foxfire 3,* concurred: "Now the very best time to dig it is after the first frost. From then till the leaves fall off of it. It's a bright yellow then, and it's a different cast of yellow from anything else in the woods, and you can tell it just as far through the woods as you can see it."

Gary suggested I look also for companion plants such a blue cohosh, a plant I didn't know, and Indian turnip, which I thought I didn't know either, but was what I called jack-in-the-pulpit. Other companion plants include trillium, black cohosh, mayapple, and bloodroot. Burkhart said you're almost 100 percent guaranteed to find ginseng if you look down and see jack-in-the-pulpit and rattlesnake fern. "That's the trifecta of right growing conditions," he said. Some refer to rattlesnake fern as "pointer fern" or "sang fern" because the fern is supposed to point directly to ginseng. Others say that's a myth.

Here on the farm, ginseng grows under sugar maple, white ash, basswood, and tulip poplars, the latter of which we have in abundance on a north-facing slope. McGraw said the tulip canopy has gaps, which allows some sun on the forest floor. Ginseng doesn't like full shade.

"Good eye," Gary said, when, finally, after seventy-five minutes, I located my first ginseng—a two-pronger, not particularly impressive—about four inches off the ground. We did not dig it up. Then Emily found a big three-pronger with five red berries, and Gary dug that root, giving the plant a "wide birth" so as not to damage it. But we had to watch out for tigers. Chinese legend says the root can escape diggers by morphing into a tiger, a man, or a bird, that the root is the devil, and hunters might perish digging it. We were safe, so far.

Gary took a bite. "Bitter," he said.

"Like a not very good carrot," I said.

State law says you can't pick ginseng until it has a minimum of three prongs, and the berries are red. Never harvest out of season. A license is required if the intent is to export. Good stewardship practices are numerous, including planting the seeds at the harvest site, three-quarters of an inch to an inch deep, and leaving some mature plants to insure propagation.

McGraw has studied thirty wild populations for twenty years and said ginseng, rated "vulnerable" in Pennsylvania, is in decline. "Unless we find a way to interact with the plant in a sustainable fashion, it's on its way to extinction," McGraw said. The top three stressors are overharvest, the overpopulation of white-tailed deer, which eat the plant, and climate change. Poachers are an issue also, even though the plant is regulated by the U.S. Fish and Wildlife Service and since 1975 has been protected under CITES (Convention on International Trade in Endangered Species of Wild Fauna and Flora). Invasive species such as burning bush, Japanese barberry, and multiflora rose can crowd out native plants such as ginseng.

McGraw believes ginseng is a resource worth preserving—and not just for humans. "I'd like to put in a plug for its value for wildlife," he said. "The wood thrush loves ginseng fruit. At the end of the year, we see wood thrushes coming to fruits that turn red. They regurgitate and disperse the seeds." He wondered if songbirds might get an energy boost from ginseng for the long migration to Central America.

My beleaguered husband might get a boost from ginseng too. Colonel William Byrd, in his 1841 book *Containing the History of the Dividing Line Betwixt Virginia and North Carolina*, wrote of ginseng root: "It cheers the heart of a man that has a bad wife, and makes him look down with great composure upon the crosses of the world."

Stinging Nettles

Of wet and wildness?
Let them be left, O let them be left,
wildness and wet;
Long live the weeds and the wilderness yet.
                              —FROM "INVERSNAID"
                    BY GERARD MANLEY HOPKINS

WHAT IS A WEED?

A plant in the wrong place is a common definition, or as Ralph Waldo Emerson said, "a plant whose virtues we haven't yet discovered." But nettles— weeds to most of us—have virtues long discovered.

Nettles have been used as dye and livestock feed, and made into loin-cloths, WWI uniforms, sails, rope, fishnets, baskets, and bow strings. Samuel Pepys wrote in his diary of eating very good nettle porridge and legend has it that Julius Caesar's troops rubbed themselves with nettles to stay awake during battle.

I too rub my fingers along the plant's stinging hairs when I hike in the woods, but I'm not trying to stay awake. I'm hoping for an anti-inflammatory effect for my arthritic hands—unwittingly imitating a Native American tra-dition called urtication, or whipping oneself with nettle branches for arthritis relief. Sadly, I've had no analgesic benefit, only pain and relentless itching, massaging my hands to soothe them—all the way home.

But Calyx Liddick, an herbalist and ethnobotanist at Northern Appalachia School of Vitalist Herbalism and Ecology in South Central Pennsylvania, has had success with urtication with her patients. For me to see positive results, she said that I might have to ingest one to two cups a day of a nettle infusion and perhaps use other herbs as well. "One method may work better for one person than another," she said.

An arthritis remedy is only one of nettle's many medicinal uses, which, according to the American Botanical Council, was used by Ancient Egyptians

for arthritis and back pain, by Greek physicians such as Hippocrates (460–370 BCE) for more than sixty ailments, and has been a folk remedy since ancient times, treating gangrene, tumors, dog bites, allergies, kidney function, chronic fatigue, bladder inflammation, and broken bones. Nettles aren't just a folk remedy, either; clinical studies have looked at nettle's effect on Benign Prostatic Hyperplasia, diabetes, osteoarthritis, urinary tract infections, and hay fever. One double-blind trial of patients with Osteoarthritis, Rheumatoid Arthritis, and Ankylosing Spondylitis found urtication resulted in decreased disability and pain.

Pennsylvania has three types of nettle—our native wood nettle (*Laportea canadensis*) and two species of *Urtica*, or stinging nettle: native *Urtica gracilis* and non-native *Urtica dioica*. (Urticaceae, the family name, is from the Latin *urere*—"to burn.") Wood nettle and stinging nettle are each two to six feet high, with serrated leaves and inconspicuous greenish flowers, but the difference is that wood nettle leaves are alternate whereas stinging nettle's are opposite. Wood nettle is usually found in rich soil in the woods and stinging nettle in "waste places," where the ground has been disturbed, such as roadsides, ditches, fields, and riverbanks. Both plants have tiny, stinging hairs called trichomes, meaning that wood nettle, while not called stinging nettle, stings too.

Nettles are one of the first plants to come up in spring—March or April in western Pennsylvania—considered a spring tonic or blood cleanser. Tender, young, shoots are best for cooking, and while many advise not to pick nettle barehanded or to eat the plant raw, some experts I spoke to do exactly that.

In Dorset, England, there's a yearly raw nettle eating contest, where, in 2019, the male and female winners ate, in one hour, fifty-two and thirty-four feet, respectively. The winner, from best I can discern, gets a trophy, bragging rights, and an upset stomach.

I wore gloves when snipping stinging nettle leaves near our pond, then stir-fried them like spinach—once dried or cooked, nettle loses its sting—and brewed nettle tea. Recipes are easy to find for nettle soup, pesto, pizza, ravioli, and frittatas. I've made nettle salve by drying the leaves, soaking them in olive oil, and adding melted beeswax. To nourish the plants in my vegetable garden, I've concocted a nitrogen-rich nettle fertilizer.

Virtues indeed!

"I don't know any herbalist who doesn't love nettles," Liddick said. "Nettles are one of the most nutrient dense herbs that we have." The plant is full of vitamins, minerals, and antioxidants, and she finds it "way tastier than spinach." There can be contraindications, however. People who take blood thinners should not take nettle, she said, because it's high in vitamin K, nor those with obstructive urinary stones "because nettles have a tendency to flush the urinary tract out—great for preventing infections, not great if there is a blockage," she said. "Of course, always check with a doctor before eating," she said.

Since most people regard stinging nettle as a weed and want to eradicate it, Liddick gets the non-native *Urtica dioica* for free. "There's all this hate surrounding invasive species," she said, but offered a solution: "Use them!" Pulling the weed won't harm the environment, harvesting helps keep the numbers in check, and doing both makes us better stewards of the environment. "I can't advocate enough for people to get to know the invasive species and weeds around them."

I asked Adam Haritan, a forager and educator whose company, Learn Your Land, teaches classes on plant, tree, and mushroom identification, how to recognize nettles in the wild. "It's a cliché, but you feel it before you see it," he said. Haritan prefers to eat nettles early in the season when the leaves are just unfurling. He pinches off the tender tips of leaves barehanded, then eats them raw. "If you fold it like a taco, you probably won't get stung," he said. He's found relief from allergies by sipping tea or a tincture of nettle and vodka.

Nettle's new growth is vibrant green, tinged with a bit of red or purple, and the plant "looks like mint." he said. "If you look closely, you can see the tiny stinging hairs." Keep in mind when foraging, though, "to learn whether or not a plant is native. Is it prolific or endangered? Ask yourself what impact you'll have by harvesting this plant." He agrees with Liddick that we need to appreciate the plants in our backyards. "I don't think we give the land we live on enough credit. We always want to go to exotic places."

Botanist Steve Grund from the Western Pennsylvania Conservancy said the hairs on the stinging nettle are like tiny pipettes with round caps at the tips. When the plant is disturbed, the cap breaks off and the hair bends and "squeezes acids or hormones up the hair and into the skin." Debate exists whether the irritant is formic acid (which gives ants their sting) histamine, serotonin, acetylcholine, tartaric, oxalic acid, or a combination. "We know some of the chemicals that are in there," he said, "but no one has really narrowed it down or determined which or what combinations are responsible for the skin reaction." But if you do get stung, Grund has an antidote: jewelweed, a succulent, two to five feet high, with bright orange flowers, which often grows near nettle. Squeeze the sap from the stem and rub it on the sting. Native Americans also use jewelweed as an antidote for stinging nettle and poison ivy; Liddick uses dock and plantain as well.

If you can't identify a plant in your woods, don't assume it's not important for wildlife, Grund said. "If we want to protect our native species, we have to protect their habitats. Learn to appreciate the weed that stings, learn what it's good for."

The weed that stings is an important food source for butterflies and moths in Pennsylvania, according to Pete Woods, inventory ecologist for the Western Pennsylvania Conservancy. Nettles are the only host plant used by caterpillars of the Milbert's tortoiseshell butterfly and a primary food source for caterpillars of the red admiral butterfly. The plant is one of several used by the eastern comma and question mark butterflies. Pennsylvania has two moths that eat only wood nettle: large hypena and the sordid hypena. "Even though people love to hate nettles, they have an important role," Woods said. "Not every plant has this many creatures that specifically depend on it."

I've never known a fellow who had "a favorite gall," as Woods does, but his favorite gall grows on wood nettle, which he described as a "translucent, round, green jewel," inside of which is a fly larvae. The fly that makes that gall, *Dasineura investita*, was only described in 2016, he said, so has no common name yet. Another gall, a fuzzy one called *Dasineura pilosa*, is specific to wood nettle also.

Why not have a truce then with the weed that stings? Praise its virtues, take advantage of its many attributes? For free. Shun commercial fertilizer, reject spinach from a factory farm, promote wildlife, try an alternative remedy? This spring, I'll go into the woods, pluck a cup of nettle's new growth, and infuse the leaves overnight in a quart of not-quite-boiling water. In the morning, I'll strain the liquid, heat it, sip a nettle infusion, and hope for less pain.

O let them be left!
Long live the weeds and the wilderness yet.

Ramps

At Greene County's 29th Annual Ramp Festival on a sunny Saturday in April, a party atmosphere was in full swing with crafters, wood carvers, metal workers, and a band. But the main draw was about fifteen vendors selling ramp chili, ramp sausage, ramp cookies, ramp mints, ramp butter, ramp wine, ramp hardtack, ramp pancakes, and ramp coleslaw. A bag of ramps cost $7.

"Deep fried ramps are the biggie," a volunteer said. The next most popular dish was ramp potato soup.

At another ramp festival a few miles away over the West Virginia border, I ate ramp fritters so airy and delicious I had to resist eating the entire tray.

"We dug thirty-four bushels for the festival," said one Washington county vendor at the Pennsylvania venue.

I can feel Russ Cohen flinch.

"I am a conscientious objector to chefs and the foodie world," Cohen said. He's foraged in New England for forty years and said ramps have been overharvested. The number one problem is "foodies with fat wallets"—those who collect ramps with a gold-rush mentality, pulling up hundreds of pounds, obliterating entire patches. "Ramps are now gone from places they used to grow," he said.

In 2013, *New York Magazine* offered a foodie ramp timeline. *New York Times* food critic Mimi Sheraton first mentioned a Finger Lakes organic farmer who harvested ramps in 1982. A year later, *Gourmet* magazine ran recipes for ramp tart and ramp grits souffle. By 1992, Chanterelle, a fancy NYC restaurant, had ramps on the menu, and in 2007, ramps appeared in farmer's markets, where, according to the magazine, "customers argue over the last few bunches."

But we Appalachians aren't foodies with fat wallets. We've celebrated the ramp for years, way before East Coast chefs caught on. Thirty years ago, when I discovered a hillside of ramps on our western Pennsylvania farm, my New York City friends hadn't even heard of the wild leek. (Ransom, wild leek, and wild garlic are other names for ramps.) For eighty-one years, Richwood, West Virginia, has held its "Feast of the Ransom." They claim their festival is the oldest in the state and call themselves the "Ramp Capital of the World."

Earlier still, European colonists harvested ramps, and "for that matter, native Americans got to it way before any of us," said botanist Eric Burkhart of Penn State. The American Indian Diet and Health project website claims the Cherokee treated earaches with ramp juice, the Ojibwa dried and stored ramps, the Chippewa used them to induce vomiting, and the Iroquois treated intestinal worms with the plant. Russ Cohen said Winooski, Vermont, may have gotten its name from the Abenaki word for onion or leeks, which grew along the river there, and the name Chicago might be the Menominee word for ramps: shika'ko.

Native Americans are said to have considered ramps a spring tonic, cleansing the blood after a long winter of no fresh produce. Others claim ramps have more vitamin C than an orange, contain antioxidants, are an antibiotic, can be used as a poultice for bee stings, and relieve the common cold. But Burkhart said no formal studies have confirmed any of that. Ramps simply taste good.

On our farm, ramps (*Allium tricoccum*) poke up through dead leaves in the woods in late March or early April. Along with trillium, spring beauty, common blue violet, and other perennial woodland plants, ramps share the lovely title of "spring ephemeral," the first plants to emerge in spring. Ramps range from Georgia to Canada, can be found under trees such as tulip, maple, basswood, and oak, grow in communities or clumps, and may be surrounded by companion plants like yellow trout lily, wood nettle, ginger, maidenhair fern, and black and blue cohosh.

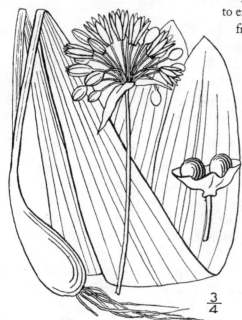

Ramps have a slightly bulbous root similar to a scallion, and two to three oblong green leaves. To me, the leaves resemble lily of the valley, and until thirty years ago ramps were part of the lily family but are now a member of the amaryllis family. As spring turns toward summer and the tree canopy fills in, ramp leaves disappear, and by June our hillside has hardly a remnant. By mid-summer, the plant sends up tiny white flowers that produce black seeds, similar to a chive, but you'd hardly know ramps had been there at all.

Many foragers sauté ramps with morels as they emerge at about the same time. But foraging can be tricky, and "you have to know what you're harvesting," Burkhart said. He mentioned false hellebore, which can grow intermixed with ramps. The two can be confused and false hellebore can "stop your heart. If you're not getting that pungent, stank smell one slice into the bulb you need a second opinion."

The ramps I dig have deep red stems, but others have green, and some foragers believe one is male and one female. "Digger's mythology," Burkhart said, explaining that ramps are hermaphrodites—both male and female. Scientists don't yet understand the color differences, but Penn State is researching the topic. Burkhart and his team are studying ramp's phytochemistry, sustainability, and the supply chain. He wants to know where ramps come from, why people use them, and the price in different markets, among other subjects.

Sustainability is a big subject with these little plants. Ramps are already deemed threatened in Quebec, and, according to the USDA, are of "special concern" in Maine and Rhode Island. Ramp harvesting was banned in the Great Smoky Mountains National Park in North Carolina and Tennessee in 2004. We have so many ramps spreading in a hollow behind our tractor shed that I didn't realize they needed protection, but just down the road from us in Westmoreland County, Burkhart said foragers have wiped out two-thirds of a slope. "Every time we go there you can see a receding line of ramps going up the canyon walls," he said. "They're getting hammered."

While the plant is considered "secure" in Pennsylvania, Burkhart said "the Laurel Highlands is among the hotspots in the state and for that reason there is some concern." A permit is required in Pennsylvania to pick ramps on public lands, for personal use only; commercial digging is outlawed. "If we aren't careful, in twenty to thirty years this slow growing plant—it takes four to five years for the plant to develop a bulb worth harvesting—will be gone," Burkhart said.

Sustainable digging means different things to different people. Cohen believes we should harvest the leaves only, taking one leaf from each plant. Burkhart prefers thinning the plant. Either way, rotating harvest sites is essential to the plant's survival. Burkhart concurred that chefs are driving ramp hysteria, especially in early spring as they want to be the first to have ramps on the menu. That forces people to harvest smaller plants that weigh less, and since ramps are purchased by the pound, more ramps are harvested.

"In mid-March it takes about five hundred plants to make a pound," but a few weeks later that number drops to one hundred or one hundred and fifty," he said.

Deer don't care for the plant, but a small fly does. The allium leafminer, an invasive insect, eats plants in the allium family. Discovered in Lancaster County, Pennsylvania, in 2015, the pest is now found in five states, but has not reached western Pennsylvania yet. The emerald ash borer, another invasive insect, is also a problem because when ash trees fall, holes are left in the overstory, allowing invasive plants to crowd out natives. For that reason, experts say after harvesting ramps to cover the hole with leaves to discourage invasive species. I'll be extra careful to do that now that I understand ramp vulnerability in my area. People are the biggest threat, Burkhart said, and if they want to save the ramp, "practice restraint."

Ramps can be difficult to dig. I've always used a large shovel, but some use a pickax, which I well understand. Others recommend a more delicate approach, such as a digging knife, a hand trowel, or a fork so as not to disturb the root system of neighboring plants.

One can grow ramps at home. A few years ago, my friend Alice and I dug some ramps on my property and she transplanted them on hers. They've multiplied. She's planted ramp seeds also. She hasn't harvested any yet, preferring to let them spread. In the meantime, she likes ramps so much she buys them at the food coop. "Ramps make any grilled meat, fish, or vegetable heavenly," she said. A favorite recipe of hers is ramp chimichurri.

"Do your homework about where ramps grow," Burkhart suggested. Ramps like moist soil in the deciduous forest, for instance, and prefer a north-facing slope. They don't grow well under conifers. But there are many other factors that go into being a successful ramp farmer.

"It's an exciting time for ramps," Burkhart said. He's pleased people have moved "away from McDonald's toward local food stuffs," and that they've recognized "the value of forest lands and developed a relationship to it." Farm-to-table, organic, seasonal, and wild foods are good to incorporate into the diet, "we just have to dig them sustainably," he said. "Some say ramps are a fad, but I don't think they're going away."

Morels

WHEN WE FIRST MOVED TO THE FARM, I KNEW WHAT PEOPLE CARRYING guns were doing on our property, but not those carrying brown paper bags. Families meandered through our woods, chatting as they went, heads bent toward the ground, scanning decayed leaves and the green growth of spring. They kneeled, put something in those bags, and walked on.

My mail carrier told me: They were searching for morels.

She'd hunted mushrooms for forty-five years and knew a good spot on our property, which she divulged, but said most people go to their graves before they reveal a favorite patch. "It's guarded like a tomb," she said. Once, in our woods, she filled two shopping bags full of morels and ran home in heavy rain before the bags broke. I've never had such luck, but have hunted the edible fungi ever since.

A morel doesn't look like a typical toadstool. Instead, its cap, which can be yellow, white, grey, beige, or black, is conical in shape with pits and ridges resembling honeycomb or sponge. Its stalk is whitish and hollow. In spring, the black morel (*Morchella elata*) emerges first, and Bob Sleigh, club identifier of the Western Pennsylvania Mushroom Club, has found his earliest morel on St. Patrick's Day—though he has legendary status in the club, finding morels when no one else can. A couple weeks later, the yellow morel (*Morchella esculenta*) appears.

Mushroom lore is rampant in our western Pennsylvania hills and locals have theories about when and how to find them: after the first warm rain, when crocus is in bloom, or when tulip leaves are the size of squirrels' ears. They swear by their favorite haunts: old apple orchards, under ash or tulip trees, by dying elms, near rotting logs. I've had the best luck under tulip poplars, but Sleigh said that's because tulip trees are the most common tree in our area to support morel growth. (The truth is, morels can be found in lawns, garden beds, or shopping center mulch, but that's hardly sporting.) In the western U.S., morels sprout after forest fires; even in the east, Sleigh advised looking under trees hit by lightning.

27

April through May is the general season, but it's not predictable. Sleigh has known morel season to last as long as six to eight weeks, and as short as one. Some people wait until tax day to go out, but if so, they may miss them all, he said. He gave me a trick: take the daytime temperature, add it to the nighttime temperature, divide by two, and when that number equals fifty and stays there a few days, it's time to head into the woods. That's because morels begin to fruit when ground temperature reaches fifty degrees. He follows web groups too, which trace morel sightings from Georgia northward in spring. One thing he called "gospel" is to start the season on a south-facing slope and work your way around the mountain as the days warm up. He believes the season's end produces the biggest mushrooms—his record is fourteen inches—which he's found under sycamores.

Morel hunters use a myriad of nicknames for the fungi not found in my mushroom guide—rubbernecks, longnecker, bigfoot, brainies, Christmas trees, butter sponge, and giant. No matter what the name, they are not easy to find. I look for shape, texture, and color, but am often fooled by half-eaten walnut shells, acorns, and the yellow-brown squawroot. (Squawroot signals the season's end, Sleigh said.) Kneel down and look uphill, Sleigh suggested—children are good at finding mushrooms, he believes, because they're so low to the ground—then turn around and see what you missed. One rule of thumb: where there's one, another is nearby.

I was told years ago to carry a mesh bag so mushroom spores could scatter as I wandered, and I do so diligently, but Michael Kuo, developer of MushroomExpert.com, and author of the book *Morels*, said, "The use of mesh bags is based on fundamental misunderstandings about how morels reproduce and how spores act," he said. Mesh bags are good for air circulation, however—don't carry mushrooms in plastic—and mesh enables dirt and bugs to fall off. To pick a morel, I was told never to pull out the root, but Sleigh plucks the entire mushroom, cuts off the bottom and buries it in another spot—so no one knows exactly where he found it. "It's a competitive hobby," he said. One of our babysitters told me to clean morels in a salty bath. "Never," Sleigh said. The flavor is in the spores, and water washes off those spores, lessening the taste. He slices morels in half lengthwise and whisks them with a soft-bristled brush.

For me, one of the delights of mushroom hunting is listening and watching the nascent world around me as spring arrives. Wildflowers bloom—trillium, jack-in-the pulpit, trout lily, dame's rocket, and wild geranium. Skunk cabbage rises in the marsh, ferns unfurl, and ramps blanket the hill behind our tractor shed. The birds are back: robins, red-winged blackbirds, the eastern phoebe. Bluebirds dart in and out of their boxes. Other mushrooms pop up too, and I imagine fairies atop them, solving fairy problems. But I don't pick them. I limit my mushrooming to morels only.

Safe foraging is crucial. In his book *The Complete Mushroom Hunter,* the late Gary Lincoff, a Pittsburgh native and author of *National Audubon Society's Field Guide to North American Mushrooms*, divides people into two camps: mycophiles, those who love mushrooms, and mycophobes, those who fear them. I'm not scared, but I *am* careful, watching in particular for the poisonous false morel, the most common of which is *Gyomitra*, with a reddish-brown cap resembling a brain, and a stalk stuffed with a cottony substance. New mushroom hunters are advised to study before picking and never eat morels raw. Join a reputable club, Sleigh suggested, or hunt with people who know what they're doing and can teach you. "We want people to be safe," he said.

I wondered why—besides my lack of skill—my mail carrier found so many more morels than I do, so I asked Kuo if climate change might be a factor. He said that question was "unanswerable in any scientific way, absent data," but that the morel's decline is fairly well documented and "probably the result of the decline of the American elm, which produced many morel fruiting bodies over a few decades as the trees died away."

When my daughter was thirteen, she liked to hunt morels with me, fry up in butter the few we found, and eat them on toast. One day we were horseback riding near the spot my mail carrier recommended, and on the edge of the woods she spotted the biggest morel we'd ever seen. It was huge and golden, and we figured there'd be more, so we trotted down to the barn, untacked the horses, put them in the field, and scurried back to the spot. It was late in the morel season, and the mushrooms were hidden under may apples in full bloom, which covered our harvest like tiny umbrellas, right out of a fairy tale.

"Found one!"

"Found one!"

We yelled it over and over to each other until we had thirty-three perfect specimens. Never had we found such a stash. But when we fried them, my daughter didn't like the toast as much—too morel tasting, she said.

My mail carrier was correct: there is something magical about that spot. But I found only two the following year, and not one in the ten years since. Perhaps others got there before I did.

Giving Thanks to Mosses

WE HARDLY NOTICE THEM. WE TROD ALL OVER THEM. MOST MOSSES DON'T even have universal common names. Moss experts are few. Yet mosses are among the most ancient of plants—the first to crawl out of the ocean and inhabit land 450 million years ago.

I wonder if that's why I feel as if I'm in an ancient land when surrounded by mosses?

Twenty-two thousand species of bryophytes—including mosses, liverworts, and hornworts—exist on every continent on the planet, from the cold of the Arctic to the heat of the desert. The only place you can't find mosses today is, ironically, in the ocean. Pennsylvania has about 580 species of bryophytes.

On my walks around the farm, I've always bent down and examined them—on the forest floor, by streams and hillsides—on rocks, logs, tree bark, and stumps. My own study of moss began by reading Robin Wall Kimmerer's beautiful meditation, *Gathering Moss: A Natural and Cultural History of Mosses*. A botanist, professor at SUNY, and a member of the Citizen Potawatomi Nation, Kimmerer brings mosses alive by combining her scientific knowledge with Native American wisdom. "I want to tell the mosses' story," she writes, "since their voices are little heard and we have much to learn from them."

Mosses are tiny, only a few centimeters tall, but play a gigantic role in our ecosystem. They collect rain, prevent erosion, and provide habitat for small invertebrates such as water bears (or moss piglets), mites, spiders, and springtails. Mosses create seed beds for larger plants to take root, keep humidity in the air, and help heal land after fires and volcanos by spreading their spores onto scorched earth. We understand now, after years of harvesting moss from peat bogs—of which Sphagnum moss is the largest component—that mosses store huge amounts of carbon and are crucial to stemming climate change. "There is more living carbon in sphagnum moss than in any other single genus on the planet," Kimmerer writes.

The more I learned about mosses, the more I marveled at them. Mosses can regenerate from broken leaves or stems, clone themselves, and dry out by 98 percent and come back to life when rains return. With no vascular system, mosses absorb water through their leaves, and with no roots, attach themselves to surfaces with hair-like structures called rhizoids. Mosses do not flower or fruit. Some are fluorescent; others resistant to insecticides. Mosses have adapted by surviving where larger plants cannot. "Mosses can live in a great diversity of small microcommunities where being large would be a disadvantage," Kimmerer writes, such as "between the cracks of the sidewalk, on the branches of an oak, on the back of a beetle, or on the ledge of a cliff."

Over the centuries, mosses have served humanity well. They've been used as insulation—in mittens, mattresses, cradles, cribs, and to chink cabins. When the 5200-year-old "Iceman" was found in a Tyrolean glacier, his boots were packed with mosses, Kimmerer tells us. Mosses are absorbent—sphagnum moss can also absorb twenty times its weight in water—and were once used as diapers and menstrual pads. Mosses are simply beautiful.

I love it when mosses naturally cover my flowerpots, and I've tried to encourage its growth with yogurt, but it is difficult. Some say to lather pots with a milkshake of moss and buttermilk, egg white, brewer's yeast or, as Kimmerer suggests, "a slurry of horse manure," which I'll try next, having a plethora of horse manure on the farm. I've tried transplanting mosses too, but not successfully. Rock loving mosses are more difficult to transplant than soil dwelling mosses, Kimmerer says, and moss must be moved to the "same conditions, the same kind of rock, light and humidity." But in the end, she writes: "I wonder if it is a kind of homesickness. Mosses have an intense bond to their places that few contemporary humans can understand."

In trying to identify mosses, I was missing a crucial piece of equipment: a jeweler's loupe. I learned that straightaway when I had the privilege of looking at mosses on the farm with Scott Schuette, a botanist and bryologist at the Western Pennsylvania Conservancy. I led Schuette first to a corner of our driveway by a stone bridge to look at a moss I particularly liked because of its blue hue. The moss looked exotic to me, but it couldn't have been more common—*Bryum argenteum*, the type nestled in the cracks of city sidewalks. Schuette retrieved his small microscope, handed it to me, and a whole new world erupted before my eyes. What had resembled a green carpet was suddenly a mass of green worms. What I had perceived as blue was actually a silver tinge on the moss's transparent tips.

Schuette loves showing mosses to people, especially in autumn when, without the diversion of flower and color, mosses are easier to spot. Then, he said, people can go back into the woods in the depths of winter and look again because mosses are still green in an otherwise brown world. Most people don't realize what they have in their own backyards, Schuette said, even

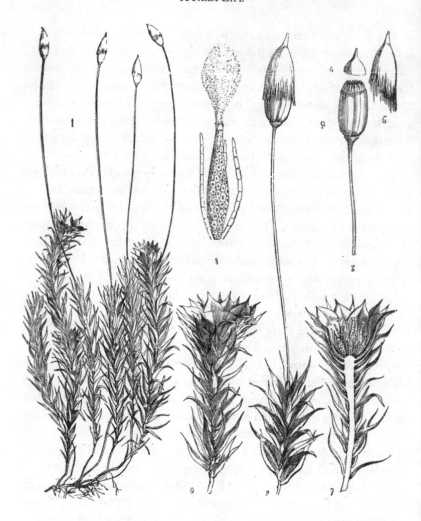

in the city. "Their minds are blown. They say, 'I had no idea.' It's great to show that to people, they slow down, take time, and look."

We walked around the edge of the pond and came upon a moss that through the microscope looked like a miniature Christmas tree. Schuette called it pinetree or tree moss, but Robert Klips's field guide, *Common Mosses, Liverworts, and Lichens of Ohio*, called it American tree moss—*Climacium americanum*. We were in its ideal habitat, on a pathway near water. I asked if walking on it harmed it, and Schuette said no, but walking on it does keep its growth at bay. Then we found *Bryoandersonia illecebra*, whose branches looked round under the microscope. Schuette called it worm moss, but the book called it spoonleaf moss.

We put our discoveries into small, brown paper bags and wrote the Latin names on top.

If mosses have benefited humans, how have we helped them? "There's not a lot of conservation effort," Schuette told me. "They aren't charismatic like elephants or lions." Humans return the favor by collecting moss for commercial purposes—up to a million pounds a year moss buyers report, according to Penn State—for horticulture use and in arts and crafts. Forty-one percent of it is collected from Appalachia by "mossers," an old Appalachian practice. We ship moss to forty countries. Irresponsible harvesting threatens not only moss populations, but lichen, fungi, and ferns. Creatures like salamanders are often harvested in the process. Schuette testified in a Pennsylvania moss poaching case against a man in Central Pennsylvania accused of stealing eighteen feed sacks of moss in a public forest. Rules exist about which mosses can be harvested, how, and where, but Schuette prefers none be taken at all as businesses now exist that grow mosses commercially.

Most animals don't eat mosses, Schuette said, because of low nutrition and phenolic compounds. "Mosses aren't inedible, they just not delectable." Reindeer, deer, or bear might eat them, he said, but only when other food sources aren't available, or when eating something else such as blueberries or cranberries. Kimmerer, however, tells the story of a bear that ate moss. The moss passed through the bear's digestive track whole and Kimmerer wonders if bears purposely eat moss to avoid defecating during hibernation.

I thought we'd travel to the far reaches of the property where for weeks I'd been making mental notes of mosses to show Schuette, but after an hour and a half we'd found so many mosses—a dozen species on just a few boulders—that we'd hardly moved from the pond. "A nice little microclimate," he said. On the roof of my writing cottage Schuette identified *Hedwigia ciliate*, which Klips's field guide confirmed is usually associated with boulders in the woods, but also "makes an appearance on old roof shingles." On a rain barrel he showed me *Hygroamblystegium varium*, described in Klips's book as "dainty," but offered no common name.

"That's your first liverwort," Schuette said to me, pointing out the fuzzy *Ptilidium pulcherrimum*—or naugehyde liverwort—on the stonewall around the riding ring. "A whole ecosystem potentially lives here," he said, including centipedes, millipedes, ants, beetles, slugs, and snails. We found a moss I had wanted to show him—which I'd given the common name of fern moss because it looked like a cluster of tiny squashed ferns—*Thuidium delicatulum*. Klips's field guide allowed that "newcomers [such as myself] to botany can be forgiven for trying to look up delicate fern moss in a fern book." We also found a moss that does have a universal common name: *Polytrichum*, "many hairs" or haircap moss, widespread and common.

"What's in a name?" Shakespeare asked. In the case of bryophytes, a whole lot of letters. Who can blame Kimmerer's students for begging for shorter names so that mosses are easier to learn? How about memorizing this "mouthful of a name" as Schuette called a tiny liverwort—1.5mm wide that grows in bogs—*Fuscocephaloziopsis loitlesbergeri*?

I was charmed by a moss we found that Schuette described as wearing a little stocking cap, so much easier to remember than *Orthotrichum ohioense*. Still, what fun I had bandying about our invented common names. Klips's field guide called *Dicranum scoparium* little brooms, but I called it little troll hair, and Schuette called it bad-hair-day-moss. No matter the name, what a magical, miniature world Schuette helped me discover under my feet.

At the end of Kimmerer's book, she gives thanks to mosses for helping other plants and animals to flourish. Tree seedlings thank mosses for places to sprout; fungi for moisture; birds for nest-building materials; and insects for habitats for their larval stages. Now that I have met mosses, I give thanks to them too. "The patterns of reciprocity by which mosses bind together a forest community offers us a vision of what could be," Kimmerer writes. "They take only the little that they need and give back in abundance." She wishes humans would do the same.

BIRDS

Chimney Swifts

At first, I thought they were bats and I was thrilled because bats are nearly nonexistent on our farm now. But something wasn't quite right. How high they flew. The sounds they made. Barn swallows maybe? But barn swallows dart in and out of our outbuildings all day. They don't just fly near the farmhouse at dusk.

These little five-inch birds were neither bats nor swallows, but chimney swifts.

A few swooped out of the sky toward the house each night last summer when my husband and I ate dinner on the porch. We heard them before we saw them. More arrived, then what seemed like hundreds, squawking loudly. They circled the chimney, and like fighter jets landing on aircraft carriers, tried to position themselves just right. Some hit the entrance on the first try, but others aborted and took another pass. I stood and watched them. Round and round they went, a funnel cloud of hundreds of birds, at that moment between light and darkness, when the pines are backlit against a fading sky.

Later, walking across the lawn after closing the chicken coop, I noticed six swifts still circling, then three; all but one had made it into the chimney. I heard the rise of the nighttime chorus of bullfrogs, katydids, and crickets, and by the time I saw the evening star and fireflies twinkling around the apple trees, all the swifts were tucked in safely for the night.

And tucked in they were—into our uncapped, unlined, nineteenth-century stone flue—the perfect spot for chimney swifts, unusual birds in so many ways. They bathe on the wing, don't roost in trees, seldom touch the ground, and cannot perch like normal birds; instead, they cling to vertical surfaces with their claws. Brownish gray with pale throats, stubby necks, and short square tails, they have long curved wings that cross an inch or so at their tail feathers, which, when stretched out, have a wingspan of about twelve inches. "A cigar with wings" was how Roger Tory Peterson described them.

Males and females are identical in appearance and there's equality in the chimney swift world as each takes responsibility for rearing the young.

"There's a rule of thumb with birds, the more the male and female look alike, the more they share the nesting duties," said Jim Bonner, executive director of the Audubon Society of Western Pennsylvania. During breeding season, which takes place in our area from May to July, chimney swifts build cup-shaped nests of small twigs glued together with saliva. Only one nesting pair is allowed in a chimney during that time, although they occasionally accept non-breeding birds that may act as nannies to help raise chicks.

Years ago, when these birds were called American swifts, they nested in cliffs, caves, and hollow old-growth trees, but the clearing of forests made such spots scarce. So they took instead to man-made structures such as chimneys, and in the late nineteenth century, their name was changed to chimney swift. Now these little acrobats have new problems. Houses are built without chimneys or chimneys are capped or lined with metal, making it impossible for the birds to grab hold of the sides. Although they are protected by the

Migratory Bird Treaty Act, chimney swifts are often killed inadvertently or purposely by homeowners, and in the last fifty years, the chimney swift population has declined 72 percent nationwide and 52 percent in Pennsylvania. In 2010, The International Union for Conservation of Nature classified them as "near threatened." With this in mind, and since swifts often mate for life and return to the same spot each year, my husband and I decided we'd allow them continued use of our chimney. Our house is now theirs.

Other factors have contributed to the birds' decline, such as fewer native plants and a decrease in bugs due to pesticides. Fewer bugs could really matter to birds that spend all day on the wing eating five thousand to six thousand insects a day, including gnats, fleas, moths, mayflies, mosquitos, and beetles. Still, "we don't have a good understanding of the diet of adult birds," said Luke DeGroote, avian research coordinator at Powdermill Nature Reserve. He cited a report showing that 76 percent to 82 percent of insects in Germany have declined in the last twenty-seven years, and said ornithologists are worried how this will affect aerial insectivores. "A hot topic now," he said.

Overall, ornithologists know surprisingly little about this mysterious bird. The birds' "daily elevation profile not known," states Cornell's Birds of North America website. No one knows exactly how they choose roosting sites, how they forage, or precisely where they winter. They're difficult to study for many reasons: because of their aerial behavior; because they nest in such enclosed places; and "they're quick, small, and travel in flocks," DeGroote said. Powdermill will use new technology called nanotags to better understand how diet, landscape, and pesticides affect chimney swifts.

Why should we care about chimney swifts? "We care on different levels and for different reasons," said Bonner of Audubon. "It's the ethics and importance of protecting any living creature that makes up our ecosystem. We care about ourselves. It's an overused cliché, but they are the canaries in the coalmine. On another level, they're just great birds, fun, playful, beautiful to watch, and there's something very special about a bird that returns each summer from South America to share our homes with us."

Mary F. Day, an early observer of chimney swifts, would have likely agreed. In her 1899 article "Home Life in a Chimney," published in *Bird Lore Magazine*, she wrote about observing nesting swifts in her New Jersey home by placing a mirror in the chimney and watching the birds through a stovepipe opening covered with black fabric. "Although the room was used as a bedchamber throughout the summer the swifts never seemed to be annoyed by the close proximity of their human neighbors," she wrote. "They were of a trustful disposition and soon became accustomed to being watched."

Women, it seems, championed the tiny bird in the nineteenth and early twentieth centuries. Men did too, of course, but it was the perfect union between women and birds because chimney swifts came out of the woods and landed into the homes of smart, curious, and bird-loving women. Althea R. Sherman was another. She wrote "Birds of an Iowa Dooryard," and in 1915 designed and had built the first chimney swift's tower—a wooden, twenty-eight-foot-high, nine-foot-square tower with windows, doors, peep holes, and a three-story staircase. Bonner called Sherman "one of many women who have been instrumental in driving avian research and conservation—many of whom are not known to the public."

Sherman's *Chimney Swift Journals* comprised more than four hundred pages of handwritten notes and are "the basis of everything we now know about what she called 'the home life of the chimney swift,'" wrote Paul and Georgean Kyle in *Chimney Swifts: America's Mysterious Birds Above the Fireplace.* The Kyles also run the Chimney Swift Conservation Association in Austin, Texas, "our effort to draw attention to the plight of these highly beneficial yet often maligned birds," Georgean Kyle said. Yet another woman, Margaret Whittemore (1897–1983) observed chimney swifts, raised orphaned birds, and wrote *Chimney Swifts and their Relatives*, a seminal book on the subject.

I have not built a chimney, conducted scientific research, or raised orphans. I've only observed chimney swifts on a western Pennsylvania farm, and occasionally rescued birds that fell out of the chimney and flew around the house. But it's nice to feel part of this long line of women who care about birds. Last autumn, I paid close enough attention to know that our chimney swifts had departed by September 20, when they signaled to each other that it was time to gather together and migrate en masse to Ecuador, Peru, Chile, or Brazil—or maybe Columbia. Our chimney swifts will be back in our area by April, and you can be sure I'll be looking out for them, awaiting their return, keeping the chimney clear.

A Belted Kingfisher

ONE SUMMER DAY NOT LONG AGO, I SAT ON THE FRONT PORCH OF OUR
farmhouse. It's a log house, built about 1860 and added onto over the
years—a happy home where my husband and I have raised two children and a
menagerie of animals: horses, cows, goats, a lamb and a turkey, bunnies, chickens, and the requisite dogs and cats. We have a vegetable garden, hayfields,
riding trails, and a barn. Below the house is a small pond with a wooden dock,
on which sits a red Adirondack chair.

That morning I noticed something draped across the front of the chair.
Something dark. Perhaps a sweatshirt left by my husband, who likes to run in
the woods in the early morning and often sits there with the dogs to cool off.
Or maybe someone had forgotten a towel after a swim. I walked downhill to
investigate—across the lawn, under the gnarled apple trees, through the gate
in the stonewall, by the metasequoia and the maple. As I got closer, I could
tell that the object was neither sweatshirt nor beach towel, but I still couldn't
tell what it was. Bluish gray, with a curious black-and-white pattern on it, the
dark mass was in crisp contrast to the bright red chair.

It was a perfect specimen of a belted kingfisher (*Megaceryle alcyon*).

My husband and I have an odd affinity for predominately black and-white
(or dark blue) birds: oystercatchers, magpies, arctic terns, black-winged stilts,
loons, auks, and great black-backed gulls. I'm not sure where that comes
from—probably birding trips early in our marriage before the children were
born—but we have framed prints of these birds in our bathroom. By odd
coincidence, one of our favorites is the belted kingfisher with its distinctive
rattling call, prominent bill, and its ability to dive from great heights—twenty
to forty feet—straight down into water to catch prey, usually fish and crayfish.
I particularly love its wildly crested head—to me, an amusing punk hairdo—
which gives the bird a confident air. And I like the fact that the belted kingfisher is one of the few birds where the female is more colorful than the male.

My visitor was about a foot long, with white bars on its black wingtips,
white polka dots on black tail feathers, and a rust-colored ring around its

neck. Somehow it had achieved a direct bull's-eye through the chair's vertical slats, a narrow seven-eighths of an inch. Its wide wingspan resembled an
elaborate Native American headdress splayed across the front of the chair. On
the back of the chair, only the bird's head and long bill were visible.

"I've never heard of a bird getting stuck in a chair," said Luke DeGroote,
avian research coordinator at Powdermill Nature Reserve in Rector. I asked
him what might have happened. Was the belted kingfisher hunting something and lost its direction, diving and got confused? How could it not have
seen a bright red chair? DeGroote surmised that the bird was being chased
by a predator, probably a raptor—most likely in our area a merlin, peregrine
falcon, or a smaller hawk such as a goshawk, broad-wing, or Cooper's. He
identified the bird as a young female hatched that spring, as indicated by its
rust-colored belt and neck feathers. I gave the specimen to Powdermill, hoping it might be used for education or research.

Haunted by the image of the bird's demise and curious to know more, I
sent photographs to the Cornell Lab of Ornithology in Ithaca, New York.
Kevin McGowan, an online education specialist there, said he didn't think the
belted kingfisher's skull would have fit directly through such a small opening
in the slats. Instead, he said, the bird must have been attacked directly above
the chair, or collided with the chair higher up, and slipped down into the gap.

From Cornell's websites, I learned that belted kingfisher males fiercely defend their territories during the breeding season and that females are often more aggressive and territorial than males. Strong competition has been observed between females "in which a younger bird was driven from her territory and her eggs dumped." Was this the fate of our bird?

Belted kingfishers build nests by burrowing into banks—streams, ponds, even roadsides. Its eyes are closed when it hits the water, and after mating, the male gives a show near the water's surface—gliding and diving, then recovering, extending its wings, and flashing the white on its feathers. During mating season, they are monogamous. Immature birds have stomachs with a high acid content in order to digest fish scales and bones, but by the time they leave the nest their stomach chemistry changes, and they regurgitate food. Having just seen the downfall of one female, and knowing that many bird species are in decline, I worried that our belted kingfishers might be endangered, but DeGroote said no. "They're pretty abundant, and good at what they do," he said.

The kingfisher, of which there are three varieties in North America and about ninety worldwide, is full of legend. In some Native American tribes, the kingfisher symbolizes peace and prosperity. In Greek mythology, when Alcyone discovers that her husband has drowned, she hurls herself into the sea in grief, and the gods turn her and her husband into kingfishers. Alcyone's father, Aeolus, king of the winds, stops the wind from blowing for seven days on either side of the winter solstice, a period known as Halcyon Days, or, according to the Cambridge English Dictionary, "a very happy or successful period in the past."

Sitting on my porch, I have heard the rattle of the belted kingfisher many times since—by the pond, at the edge of the woods, near the stream deep in the forest. I have seen them dart across the pond from one tree branch to another. I have searched the pond's bank for burrows but have found none—so far. Especially in these uneasy times of political rancor and social unease, I will take the lead of Native Americans and believe that western Pennsylvania's belted kingfishers are predicting peace and posterity to this farm—and to us all.

Raising Chickens

BUFF COCHINS: SOLD OUT. BARRED ROCKS: SOLD OUT. LIGHT BRAHMAS: Sold out. Not a hen of my choice available this year from Murray McMurray, the hatchery in Iowa where I've ordered peeps for thirty years. My flock, which usually numbers around thirty birds, had dwindled to nine, so I needed layers, particularly of green and blue eggs, and a Cochin rooster. But due to the coronavirus, suddenly everyone wanted to be a chicken farmer.

I had no choice but to hatch my own, so I separated a large, orange, furry-footed Buff Cochin rooster and four hens, put them in a horse stall in the barn with food, water, and nesting boxes—and hoped for a broody hen. Little did I know how invested I'd become in the trials and tribulation of raising chicks.

When my daughter was young, we perused the Murray McMurray catalogue filled with chickens speckled, frizzled, spangled, booted, bearded, muffled, penciled, silver laced, combed, and high tailed, and she picked the oddest, rarest breeds she could find. One of her favorites was the White Crested Black Polish, which she named Cheffy because its white hair stuck straight up, resembling a toque. We always included extra Buff Cochin pullets—and a Buff Cochin cockerel—because those are my husband's favorite. And we've had runner ducks, African geese, and a turkey.

"It's been a year," said Tom Watkins, owner, with his wife and father-in-law, of Murray McMurray, which has raised fowl since 1917 and also sells guinea hens, pheasants, peafowl, quail, and partridge. The year 2020 started out similarly to 2019, he said, until one week in March when calls went from the usual five or six hundred a day to sixteen hundred. "An astronomical amount," he said. Egg layers and meat chickens were flying out of incubators for customers who feared food shortages, wanted to entertain and home-school children, or simply desired to know their food's origin. The hatchery usually sells a million birds a year; this year, it expects to sell 2.5 million.

The company ships birds from January through October. In colder months, the minimum is twenty-five (peeps keep each other warm during shipping) but by April, some breeds are available in groups of fifteen or fewer. Chicks can survive without food for seventy-two hours because they are still digesting the yolks of their eggs.

My daughter and I would drive to the post office and pick up what she called "the chirping box," filled with day-old peeps, and put them in a large, wooden cage with food and a heat lamp. The peeps grew quickly, scurrying across the barn floor, the children mesmerized, trying to identify which breed was which. (My daughter remembers our cat, sitting on the wire top, being rather mesmerized too . . .) But the journey can be difficult, and every year we lost a few, either upon arrival or a few days later. Still, Murray McMurray's success rate at hatching and keeping peeps alive was far better than mine.

Some years we didn't get the chickens we ordered, such as when eight cute peeps grew into fighting cocks, chased hens across the yard, attacked, and killed them. I hated doing it, but I rounded them up, had them slaughtered at the meat packer, and made chicken broth. Watkins admitted the fault may have been theirs, but explained that all peeps go through the Memphis airport, and if a box falls open and peeps run around, they get thrown into any available box. Customers have remarked receiving ducks or turkeys they didn't order, he said. "It's not unheard of to mix things up."

Back at our barn, no hen would sit. "Poultry geneticists have done a great deal to eliminate the natural tendency for laying birds to become broody," wrote Leonard S. Mercia in *Raising Poultry the Modern Way*. Luckily, Buff Cochins are a broody breed, so I was hopeful. To entice the hens, I placed straw in the nesting box and gathered the eggs into a circle, making the surroundings look suitably nest-like.

Human folly. No hen wanted any part of it.

Each of our chickens has had its own personality. Buff Cochins are gentle giants, bantams small and feisty, crested varieties spacey. When Cheffy's crest got wet and hair covered her eyes, she spun in circles and didn't know which way to the coop. Watkins explained why: the skulls of crested varieties don't close until six weeks old, allowing hair to grow through the top of their heads. While fun to look at, they're "kind of dumb," he said. One of my favorite breeds is the Speckled Sussex, friendly and curious, always peeking into my scrap bucket to check out the day's offerings.

Thirteen breeds of chickens existed in 1868, when, according to *Storey's Guide to Raising Chickens*, by Gail Damerow, Charles Darwin published a chicken inventory. Today, there are fifty-one breeds of large chickens and sixty-two breeds of bantams, David Adkins of the American Poultry Association told me. Hens lay eggs every twenty-five hours, and egg color generally corresponds to a chicken's earlobes (try locating a chicken earlobe). White-lobed chickens lay white eggs and those with red earlobes lay brown.

Eggs have a coating called a bloom, a barrier against bacteria, so homegrown eggs ideally shouldn't be washed until ready to eat, though I can't do it.

We've had chickens fly the coop, easy prey for the fox, and chickens that roosted in trees at dusk—owl food. When the children were young, we played "chicken lax" at sunset, reaching up into the branches with lacrosse sticks to nudge them out of the tree and into the coop. We've had chickens with crooked toes, crossed beaks, mean roosters who tried to use their spurs, roosters who fought each other, and some strange hens.

Cheffy was one strange hen—she crowed. "We have reports of hens that take on rooster attributes," Watkins told me. "It's not unheard of for a hen to crow." Sometimes hens with no roosters take on the male role—but we've always had roosters. Old or diseased hens may have underdeveloped ovaries, allowing testosterone to enter the system and the hen to crow. Or perhaps Cheffy was a weak rooster. Sexing chickens, Watkins said, is a difficult and tedious task, and Murray McMurray hires professional sexers to do the job. (Vietnam, he told me, has the only technical college in the world that gives degrees in that subject.) The hatchery guarantees 90 percent accuracy, though he believes the numbers are closer to 95 to 98 percent.

One of our hens finally got broody. Then another hen climbed into the same box and pulled four eggs toward her. Mama Hen pulled them back

and ended up sitting on fourteen eggs. One of my manuals said twelve eggs is maximum, but Cochin hens are wide-breasted, and she easily covered her clutch, so I let her be.

I became a mother hen of sorts myself, checking Mama Hen multiple times a day, bringing additional kitchen scraps, keeping the pen extra clean, and spending more time than usual with the flock. Sometimes I just stood in a corner of the horse stall and watched: the rooster sound asleep, chickens grooming themselves, hens squawking and nipping at each other. One day I saw a hen facing the wrong way in the nesting box. She clucked and strained and laid a large brown egg right in front of my eyes.

Chicken sounds have become such an integral part of this farm that I cannot imagine life without them. I love hearing roosters crow at dawn and am always amused when cockerels learn to crow—a weak facsimile at first, sometimes just the cocka-doodle or just the doo. Eventually they put it all together, but no two crows are alike. The clucking of egg laying goes on all day, and of course, there's the alarm cry when a predator is nearby. Our younger dog recognizes this sound as well, lifts her head and races across the lawn, jumps the stream, and runs up the hill to chase the fox. She's the great chicken protector, even though the first thing she did the day we brought her home as a puppy was to kill a chicken.

One day, when I was alone, I heard the alarm sound, ran out, and quickly shut the chickens inside the coop. I walked the exterior of the fence to make sure the fox was gone, and there, in the corner of the fenced-in area, sat a large red fox. Luckily my neighbor returned at just the right moment, because it took two of us to maneuver the fox out without it attacking any chickens.

Poor chickens do have a plethora of creatures after them: owls and hawks from above, rats tunneling below, opossum hiding in the coop with them, fox, raccoon, mink, snakes, fishers, dogs, and cats. Owls take the head and neck, fishers kill purely for sport, snakes eat eggs and chicks and leave no trace. "Everything likes chicken," Watkins joked.

New chicken farmers should choose large breeds, Watkins advised, such as Rhode Island Reds, Barred Rocks, and Buff Orpingtons— "the beginner's best friends." Keep the coop clean and give them plenty of space, he said, and be aware of a common disease called coccidiosis, an internal para-site, which thrives in wet bedding in heat and humidity. My neighbor got salmonella from her peeps, so always wash hands after handling them, and Watkins reiterated CDC rules that no one under five handle chickens—and don't kiss them.

Waiting for the peeps to hatch seemed interminable to me and must have felt more so to Mama Hen. In the twenty-one days it takes to hatch peeps, brooding hens typically lose 20 percent of their body weight, and leave the nest for only fifteen to twenty minutes a day. Each time I checked on her, she looked thinner and more disheveled. She pecked at me viciously when I removed her from her nest to check on her clutch.

Then one day, right on schedule, I walked into the stall and saw a tiny, beautiful yellow chick. The peep knew exactly which hen was its mama and stayed closed at first, but eventually ventured out and learned to eat and drink, throwing its little head back when it did. Somehow new life in the time of Covid-19 seemed extra joyous.

I candled some of the remaining eggs and removed those I thought weren't viable, but on my way to the compost pile I heard a chirp in the box so promptly returned it. I was indeed a novice chicken farmer. A few days later when I lifted Mama Hen off the nest again, I saw pipping and heard peeping sounds through another shell; mother and baby were communicating to each other even before the little one was born. But the next day, what looked like a perfectly healthy chick didn't move, as if its legs didn't work properly. My daughter was at the farm then and she and I contemplated removing the peep but decided Mother Nature knew best. The next day it was dead, seemingly crushed.

"Generally, you are better off in the long run to let Mother Nature take her own course," said Adkins from the American Poultry Association, but now, of course, I wish I'd tried something.

I was in the barn at six o'clock the next morning checking on another egg on which I'd seen pipping. I didn't want another one to die. But from this egg I heard no sound, and when it hatched it was barely alive and didn't look normal. A few hours later it was in the middle of the stall, dead. Two more deaths followed.

Finally, enough was enough. Mama Hen had been on the nest a week longer than necessary, and I removed all the eggs. She sprinted off the nest to eat and drink and take a dust bath. *Hallelujah,* she seemed to say.

Now our one surviving peep named Mili after my son's girlfriend, born on the same day—is healthy and adorable, racing about and sitting on Mama Hen's back or under her wing, her head only peeking out. Her legs are getting long, her feet furry, and she's growing tiny wing feathers a shade darker orange than her body. Mili is short for Milagros—our little miracle.

Carolina Wrens

WHAT MUST IT FEEL LIKE FOR A BABY BIRD TO FLEDGE? TO TAKE A LEAP (of faith?) and fly for the first time? I couldn't help but wonder one warm day when I watched a clutch of birds fly off our front porch.

I feared, however, that if I wrote about birds' feelings, I'd be accused of anthropomorphizing bird behavior—until I read the preface in *What it's Like to be a Bird*, by ornithologist and illustrator David Sibley.

> *My growing sense as I worked on this book is that instinct must moti-*
> *vate a bird by feelings—of satisfaction, anxiety, pride, etc. . . . Maybe*
> *the feeling an oriole has when looking at its finished nest is similar to the*
> *feeling human parents get when we look at a newly painted and decorated*
> *nursery. Maybe a chickadee 'sleeps well' after a good day of gathering and*
> *storing food for the winter.*

So, I'll venture to say that fledging was routine for three tiny, fuzzy-headed Carolina wrens, with their cinnamon feathers, white breasts, cocked tails, and eyebrow stripes as they emerged, one by one, from a birdhouse set atop our transom window. And I'd say it was downright terrifying for the fourth wren who really had no interest in flying at all.

I was below that transom, reading on a wicker couch, when suddenly adult wrens flitted wildy from lilac branch to flowerpot, window shutter to porch railing, pegboard to pillow, muck boots to thermometer, chirping what the American Bird Conservancy calls "harsh, scolding notes." Was it mom and dad? Perhaps. The sexes have the similar plumage, but one bird was noticeably larger, presumably the male, common for Carolina wrens.

When our children were young, we built an Irish cottage birdhouse to raise money for Powdermill Nature Reserve. The birdhouse is made of round stones painted white, with a thatched roof, a red door, and red window trim. At the auction, Valley School's art teacher, who's married to an Irishman, bid on it, which pleased me, but unbeknownst to us, my father-in-law bid higher in order to return the birdhouse to the children. It rested on the transom ledge for years, unused by birds.

Carolina wrens don't usually build nests in traditional birdhouses with small entrance holes, but instead in unlikely spots: hanging plants, mailboxes, tin cans, shirt pockets, shoes, and hats. We've had wrens nest in a hanging lantern at our front entrance, a hay rack, and a wire basket that holds my husband's horse brushes and sponges. That nest was funnel-shaped and elegantly woven with twigs, weed seeds, pine needles, moss, and decayed leaves. And who can't love a species where the male builds what the Cornell Lab of Ornithology calls numerous "nest starts," and then allows the female to choose her favorite? Bob Mulvihill, an ornithologist at the National Aviary in Pittsburgh, said our Irish cottage was "definitely funky enough to catch the eye of a Carolina wren."

I watched the first baby wren come out of the birdhouse. It rested briefly on the hole and then took a six-inch practice flight, straight up, and landed back on the shelf. The next two followed, all chattering away, and within five minutes, three wrens had crash-landed onto the couch, a side table, and the porch floor—with such thuds I couldn't believe they survived. The adults continued to fly on and off the porch indicating, I believe, which direction the

little ones should follow—around the corner toward the euonymus bushes and a rose arbor. But instead, the babies hopped around the floor between sneakers, riding boots, and a doormat. One squeezed under the screen door and into our front hall. I picked it up gently with a towel and put it back outside. It went under again. Wren chaos. One fledgling shut its eyes. How tiring this all is.

The tiny, helpless creatures were easy pickings for a predator. I kept the dogs away and thought how lucky it was the cat wasn't outside, but blue jays circled a nearby apple tree, which must have been worrisome for the parents. "All the chatter is an interesting dilemma," Mulvihill said. "On the one hand, the parents must urge the babies off the nest. But on the other hand, all that noise attracts predators, which is the last thing they want to be doing."

Finally three fledglings leapt off the porch and followed mom and dad.

A fourth wren emerged. It groomed itself, stretched out its neck with a high squeal, flapped its wings, but didn't fly. It opened its mouth and begged for food. Mom arrived, fed the baby one grub, then another. She squawked. *Let's get on with it,* she seemed to say. Then all was quiet for a while. Mom and dad had disappeared, maybe tending to the other three?

Carolina wrens, the largest wren species in the eastern U.S., are little birds, about five-and-a-half inches and eat spiders and insects such as moths, crickets, grasshoppers, beetles, flies, and caterpillars. They are monogamous and have a long breeding season, two or three broods from late March until late September. Mulvihill surmised our fledglings were from a second brood. But wrens are perhaps best known for their amazing songs. "They have so much voice for their size," Mulvihill said. "They can belt it out more than just about any group of birds."

Since the mid-twentieth century, Carolina wrens have moved northward, but harsh winters can lessen their numbers considerably. "One terrible spell of weather can decimate their population," Mulvihill said. The winter of 2015 was particularly difficult for Carolina wrens with frigid temperatures and snow and ice that covered their foraging areas. During mild winters, they rebuild. "I think what we're actually seeing is microevolution of a species in my lifetime," Mulvihill said. Climate change has resulted in winter conditions that are more survivable for the species farther north, and birds that are less cold hardy are able to survive where once they weren't, he said. "Likely a blend of the two." Carolina wrens are now permanent residents of western Pennsylvania.

Mom wren flew in again, but this time she had no food. *I'll feed you when you get off that ledge,* she appeared to say, and it wasn't just my imagination. According to the Animal Diversity Web: "Adults may decrease food deliveries to get them out of the nest." But the baby didn't seem to get the message. It still wouldn't fly. Mom came back and imitated a heavenly glide as if the baby were to copy her. To no avail. She flew onto the ledge again and gave the baby a talking to. Nothing. Another time she flew in and scared the little one, as if that might make it leap. Nope.

Mulvihill said he wasn't surprised the parents were scolding the baby bird. "They're getting annoyed and impatient," he said. "Following this brood, the female goes immediately back to nesting and the couple can't be wasting time with a fledgling that won't budge out of the nest." Wren parents need to feed and care for fledglings for at least two weeks after fledging and until they disappear from their natal territory, he told me. "It's a ton of work."

Finally, mom brought a grub, showed it to the baby, but withheld it. The problem child had forced mom to stoop to extreme measures, I thought, which took me right back to my own daughter who wouldn't sleep through the night for two-and-a-half years. Against medical wisdom, I gave her a baby bottle of milk at bedtime. Either her teeth were going to rot or she was going to lose her mother, and I opted for the former. She slept through the night. She did have a tooth abscess around age seven but has survived happily. I, on the other hand, am still tired twenty-seven years later.

The baby bird cried louder and at a higher pitch when begging for food. Finally, mom gave in and brought the biggest grub yet. The baby fell asleep.

Was the baby bird sick or propulsionally challenged? Had it hatched later than the other three? Maybe I was interfering. I'd been observing the fledglings on and off for seven hours. Perhaps the baby bird simply liked the nest, Mulvihill suggested, especially after its siblings had moved out. And some birds are just braver than others, he said. "It's a push/pull for fledglings." When I went inside to make dinner, the baby was still atop the transom.

I wondered if the parents might abandon the challenging child, but Mulvihill said no, never at this stage, though they may feel tempted. For weeks all their young were in one nice basket, he said, but now the parents have to keep track of babies scattered in different directions. "It's a trying time. The adults are pulling their feathers out!"

When I came out to watch again, the fledgling was still there. The sun was setting and it was getting dark.

The baby inched onto the ledge. It looked as if it was working up the nerve, but retreated. It flapped its wings and fell over. It had been a long, stressful day for the little fellow—and for those of us watching. Dad flew in and perched next to the baby. He seemed to show it how to push off.

The fledgling's tiny pink toes gripped the ledge. It flapped its wings, and after nearly eight long hours, the baby wren jumped off the transom. Like its siblings, it landed on the couch and then hard on the floor. But it wasted no time hopping among riding boots. It didn't go under the screen door or doze off. One flight led immediately to the next. It flew off the porch floor and landed in the grass. The last I saw it, baby Carolina wren number four was nestled in a euonymus bush, its first journey away from home, into the wild.

INSECTS
AND
ARACHNIDS

Feral Bees

To make a prairie it takes a clover and one bee,
One clover, and a bee,
And revery,
The revery alone will do,
If bees are few

— EMILY DICKINSON, 1755

I AM A FAILED BEEKEEPER.

I had two hives. One died the first year and the other lasted about five, from which I got beautiful honey, but the next year those bees disappeared. True, I didn't have much of a chance, since 40 percent of managed honeybee colonies die each year, and Pennsylvania is one of the hardest hit states, always ranking in the top five.

Honeybees are dying at a rapid rate for many reasons, including Colony Collapse Disorder (first discovered in November 2006 by a Pennsylvania bee-keeper overwintering his hive in Florida), parasites—such as varroa mites—viruses, fungi, changes in food and nesting habitats, and neonicotinoids, a broad-spectrum insecticide. Penn Environment, an environmental group, defines neonicotinoids (called neonics for short) as a deadly nerve agent that damages bees' brains and cripples their ability to learn, remember, and navi-gate. A study published in the journal *Science* revealed that three-quarters of the honey tested worldwide is contaminated with neonicotinoids, which also harm butterflies, moths, other insects, and earthworms.

Shortly after I lost my second hive, honeybees showed up in a hole fifteen feet high in a walnut tree next to our barn. I fantasized those were my bees, insisting on staying close to home, but that of course was a figment of my imagination. I tried to retrieve them by sprinkling lemongrass into a hive box—a beekeeper friend had lured bees that way—but I failed. I tried homegrown lemon balm too, which I'd read attracts bees, but that didn't work either. Still, I was happy because the bees seemed content and I loved to watch and listen to them in the early morning in the vegetable garden: buzzing loudly, flying, and foraging, gathering nectar from borage, poppies, and catmint.

The next spring, near the walnut tree, I saw something large and brown against the red blossoms and green leaves of a Japanese quince. It resembled a woman's hair net, and its weight pulled the quince branch toward the ground. As I approached, I saw it was bursting with bees, some of which were not happy when I got too close. It was a swarm, and deeper into the foliage was another. I circled at a respectable distance, mesmerized by thousands of pulsating little beings, all huddled together, deciding where to set up their next home.

Swarms occur when hives become overcrowded, explained Thomas D. Seeley in his book *Honeybee Democracy*. Two thirds of the worker bees leave with the old queen and one-third remain in the original hive with a new queen. Those that leave travel only about a hundred feet before assuming the shape of the swarm, which contains approximately ten thousand bees and weighs about three pounds. Several hundred bees leave the swarm to scout for a new place to live.

"Choosing the right dwelling place is a life-or-death matter for a honeybee colony," he wrote.

One of those scouts must have decided that the stonework on the side of our garage was suitable, and they settled in. I had two hives again, albeit of a different sort—feral bees.

The definition of a feral hive is "one that has been able to survive one winter without any management," said Margarita Lopez-Uribe, an assistant professor in the Department of Entomology at Penn State. Lopez-Uribe was conducting a citizens' science project to find and study feral bees, and John Wenzel, an entomologist and director of Powdermill Nature Reserve near our farm, heard news of my feral colonies, so asked if he might extract some of the bees to take part in the study. I agreed, of course, and he and the State College team came twice last year—in March and September—complete with veils, smokers, nets, test tubes, and dry ice. They took a sample of about fifty bees, froze them, and took them back to the lab. (The bees had to be frozen in order to preserve RNA because RNA molecules are unstable and will degrade if not frozen, Lopez-Uribe explained.) So far, they've taken samples from six cities across the state—nineteen samples from feral colonies, and eleven from managed colonies.

"Our hypothesis is that the immune system of the feral bees is better," Lopez-Uribe said. But she has to prove it.

Before her study began, the belief was that feral colonies were rare, if not gone, because of mites. But, she said, "there are more out there than we initially thought we could find." Her study has shown that feral bees have more viruses than managed colonies—in particular a two-to-four-fold higher amount of deformed wing disease, which is transmitted by mites. And she's discovered that feral bees' immune systems work harder than those of domestic bees.

So what do these results mean exactly?

One of two extremes, Wenzel said. "The obvious one is that the feral bees are sicker than managed bees. However, it also could mean the opposite, which is that the feral bees can tolerate a great deal more challenge from pathogens and keep going." Wenzel and Lopez-Uribe hope the latter is true, but they have more work to do. They'll be back again this year to fetch more bees. "Stay tuned," Lopez-Uribe said.

If, in the end, the study proves that feral bees are better equipped to fight disease, the goal is to cross breed feral and domestic bees. "If we can identify colonies with stronger immune systems that can tolerate diseases and mites better, then we can conduct local breeding programs," Lopez-Uribe said.

Wenzel agreed. "We hope that by breeding the feral bees into the lines of managed bees we can get the disease-resistant immune system into the apiary," he said. "In a way, it is similar to how many agriculturists are turning back to heirloom varieties of fruits and vegetables and away from the 'green revolution' crops that were favored for high productivity."

The following spring was cold. I was on the lookout for movement in my two feral hives, the one in the walnut tree and the other on the side of our garage. So far, not a bee, and I was getting worried. The carpenter bees were back, the yellow jackets and the wasps, but no honeybees. Feral bees, however, can take longer to become active, said Katy Ciola Evans, another member of the Penn State team who had come to our farm to collect bees, so I remained hopeful. I didn't want to be a failed beekeeper again.

Ten days later, Evans emailed me and asked if there was any movement in the hives. "Any signs of flight?" she wrote. "If not, I will mark them as dead." At the end of that sentence, she added a sad face emoji.

"Not a bee," I wrote back. It *was* sad.

She told me to keep an eye out, though. The cavity might be recolonized by another swarm, and if that happened, to let her know.

Two days later I was in the vegetable garden in the morning transplanting strawberries and missing the hum of my small companions. The fellow who helps me was rototilling. We were there at an early hour to beat the heat, but it was hot already. He took a break and went down to the barn to have a drink and a sandwich.

In the distance, I heard him yell: "The bees are back."

He'd been standing near the walnut tree, heard a scratching sound on the bark, and looked up to see a red squirrel stick its nose into the hive and run away. I hurried down from the garden, but there were so few bees, so high up, I wasn't even sure they were honeybees. I went to the house and got a pair of binoculars.

Honeybees, indeed; at least one feral hive had survived the winter. I wrote Evans right away, who said the colony "probably overwintered very tiny, and it just took a few brood cycles for it to build up enough bees to be able see them." Penn State will be back this month for another test.

Perhaps reverie, no matter how it's spelled, helped.

Fireflies

"Male fireflies are like teenage boys," said Lynn Frierson Faust, who wrote the book *Fireflies, Glow-worms, and Lightning Bugs: Identification and Natural History of the Fireflies of the Eastern and Central United States and Canada*. "Males want to be seen, as flashy as possible, advertising their fitness. Look at me, they say!" One species, for instance, *Photinus pyralis*—the Northeast's most common firefly, nicknamed the Big Dipper and the easiest for children to catch—shows off his stuff by swooping up and down in a J-shaped pattern, two-to-ten feet high off the ground, hoping a female might take note and flash back, perhaps from leaf litter below.

"A love song with light," Faust called the courtship, which she compared to bird song or frog trill.

But descending from the sky, the male is careful to land as many as six inches away from the female. "He's trying to figure out, is she real, the correct species, or will she eat me?" Faust said. Because some females, it turns out, are not looking for mates, but for dinner. *Femme fatales* is the "scientific term" used by firefly experts. "It's not all love and roses if you're a firefly," Faust said. "You have to navigate a very dangerous world, at least to find a mate."

If the male suspects she's a predator, he flies off, to try again another night. But there aren't many nights for firefly love. The firefly lifecycle includes a complete metamorphosis—egg, larvae, pupae, and adult—and adults live only three to four weeks. Their larval stage, by contrast, when fireflies burrow into the ground, lasts one to two years. And while we may call these insects fireflies or lightning bugs, "they're not flies, and they're not bugs," said John Wenzel, senior biologist at DiscoverLife.

Fireflies are beetles. ("Bug" applies only to true bugs Wenzel said, such as stink bugs or bed bugs, but has become a catch-all term.) Other cultures call fireflies glow-worms, lamplighters, belly on fire, and blinkies, among others, and across the world, fireflies are full of myth. Cambodians believe they bring good luck, while Peruvians call them the eyes of ghosts. Wenzel said legend has it that when Columbus sailed to the Dominican Republic, he saw lights in the woods he thought were people carrying candles, but they were fireflies.

"Fireflies are one of the best topics in all of natural history, if you ask me," Wenzel said. "They are a great flourish of evolution."

Like many children, I twirled across our lawn on summer evenings, net in hand, trying to catch fireflies. I put them in a grass-lined jar with an aluminum foil top, into which I'd poked holes with a fork, and placed the jar on my bedside table to prolong the enchantment as I fell asleep. Seeing fireflies is for me as powerful an association with childhood as Marcel Proust and his madeleines. And I still watch them as I drift off to sleep—only now from our sleeping porch, surrounded on three sides by what continues to feel like magic.

As a child, I thought there was one type of firefly that flew around all summer, but there are more than 2,000 species worldwide, on every continent except Antarctica, and more than 125 in the U.S., with three major flashing genera: *Photuris*, *Photinus*, and *Pyractomena*. Each has its specialty: some flash in May, others in July, some at sunset or later at night, and at varying distances off the ground. Colors vary: green, orange, yellow, or blue. Each has a different flash pattern, although some don't flash at all, and some females in the eastern U.S. can't even fly. Males are generally what we see at night. Females' "answering flash" as Faust called it, is "usually shorter, paler and simpler."

Of our western Pennsylvanian fireflies, Faust said, "You all have beautiful fireflies, a huge diversity, breathtaking." She lives in Tennessee, but has studied fireflies across Pennsylvania, including Butler County where her brother's widow lives. "You have the famous synchronous firefly, straight up the Appalachians and the Allegheny Plateau," she said, referring to *Photinus carolinas*, more abundant in the Great Smokies near her, but visible in our own backyard in the Allegheny National Forest. In June and July, thousands of courting males fly in unison, sending out six flashes followed by six seconds of darkness. Firefly experts don't really understand why they synchronize.

At least fifteen species are known in the Allegheny National Forest, including another nicknamed Chinese lantern that has a bluish-green color. Such a wealth of fireflies prompted the establishment in 2013 of the Pennsylvania Firefly Festival, one of the many firefly festivals around the world. Another Pennsylvania species, *Photuris pennsylvanica*, with its dot-dash flash pattern, is our state insect, thanks to the children in Upper Darby, Pennsylvania, who petitioned the governor in 1974. These fireflies are big, with long legs, the best flyers, carnivorous, and include the *femme fatale*.

I believe I've noticed fewer fireflies than I did as a child, and Marc Branham, associate professor of entomology and nematology at the University of Florida, said he hears that lament often. "There's a general notion that firefly numbers worldwide are in serious decline," he said. For one thing, what's called ALAN—artificial light at night—prevents males from finding mates. "Neighborhoods that are lit up all night long for sake of security really interfere with firefly behavior," Branham said. Fireflies in salt marshes and coastal plains are in danger due to sea-level rise. Habitat destruction is a huge problem, especially in subdivisions, because the soil is dug up and the larvae are underneath. "You never know you lost them," Faust said. Pollution harms fireflies and lawn and garden sprays can be lethal. Branham remarked on how many fireflies he saw on Amish farms in Ohio—because for one hundred years they've kept the soil balanced and the ecosystem healthy by rotating crops without the use of herbicides, pesticides, or fungicides.

The good news is that fireflies don't bite, sting, aren't scary or creepy-crawly, and don't harm crops, Faust said. "They are one of the few insects we are *not* trying to kill." Most people are delighted by them, and they connect us in a phenomenal way to the natural world.

"Once the sun goes down, they put on a show," Branham said.

Fireflies eat primarily in the larval stage—mostly snails, slugs, and earthworms. Faust has seen a firefly larva inject numbing venom into a cockroach and the cockroach didn't even know it was being eaten. For years, experts believed fireflies didn't eat at all as adults, but in 2014, Faust discovered fireflies sipping the sap of milkweed. Generally, though, "fireflies go from being eating specialists as larvae to being breeding specialists as adults," the late firefly expert Dr. Jim Lloyd said in Faust's book.

Fireflies have a host of defense mechanisms. "How else could you fly around advertising your location with flashing lights in a world filled with frogs, toads, bats, and birds?" Faust asked. Their bioluminescence, in addition to being a mating signal, is also a warning signal: don't eat me. They play dead, are camouflaged, and have menacing aposematic coloration of red, orange, and yellow combined with black and white. They smell and taste bad. John Wenzel ate one once, calling the flavor bitter and horrible. That taste is a cardiac toxin called lucibufagin, which has been known to kill escapee exotic pets that made the mistake of snacking on fireflies; it's surmised that eating ten could kill a human. Toads, however, must go back for second helpings as they've been seen glowing through their stomach walls. (Toads, Branham said, are known to eat distasteful things and have a bad long-term memory.) Some birds eat them, such as grosbeaks and robins, but very few; spiders are one of the creatures that gobble them up. Lucibufagins are why *femmes fatales* eat males of another species; they cannot manufacture their own defense chemicals so eat males that contain it and transfer those chemicals to their eggs and larvae.

Fireflies have been studied since the 1700s, but there's much scientists don't understand, and new species are still being discovered. Mass Audubon runs a Firefly Watch encouraging people to become citizen scientists. So go out when the temperature is 60 to 85 degrees (below 50 degrees there's no point in looking, Faust said) find a natural location, such as a park, conservation area, cemetery, farm, or forest. Study flash patterns and keep a record of what you see, where, and when. Were my children younger, I'd urge them to discover a new firefly. I may even take a twirl or two with a net this summer.

My daughter tells me she too remembers poking holes in aluminum foil and catching fireflies, but as young firefly hunters, we may have been too careless. I wasn't aware we should have kept them out of the hot sun and air conditioning, or that instead of grass we might have added moistened, unbleached coffee filters to the jar, maybe even an apple slice. We should have released them within twenty-four hours to the same location. Still, Faust, a great protector of fireflies, is adamant that children be allowed to catch them. "Please do not forbid children that lifelong, pleasurable, wondrous memory of catching fireflies on a warm summer's evening and putting them in a jar," she wrote.

If I think back to activities I wanted to share with my young children, catching fireflies would surely be one of them. Is that not childhood at its best? Unplugging from the electronic world, being outdoors on a summer evening, marveling at one of nature's wonders, sharing it together, maybe even learning something about science? I hope *their* children get to participate in this same ritual, so please, turn off the lights. Stop spraying chemicals. Save a firefly.

Spiders

FOR MOST PEOPLE, AUTUMN CONJURES THOUGHTS OF GOING BACK TO school—notebooks, pencils, erasers, and backpacks. Apple picking, perhaps, or the first frost.

I think of spiders.

When my children were young and we raced up our flagstone steps on autumn mornings to get to school by 8:10, we often delayed ourselves further by stopping to look at the spider webs along the way—webs that seemed to appear out of nowhere, webs that weren't there, or weren't noticeable, the day before. These webs resembled tiny hammocks or trapeze nets and were tacked onto the edges of the yew hedge—and there were many of them, some multi-tiered, in the boxwood too, and on the ground euonymus.

Some of our spiders were sheet weavers, the family Linyphiidae, the second largest spider family of the fifty thousand spider species in the world and thirty-five hundred in the U.S. In our area, the most common sheet weavers are the bowl-and-doily spider and the filmy dome spider. Sheet weavers are tiny, less than three-eighths of an inch, and hang upside down on the underside of their webs and wait for insects such as gnats, flies, aphids, and mosquitoes. They bite them with their fangs, pull them down through the web, and wrap them in silk to eat later.

These spiders also "balloon," or float on long strands of gossamer silk produced by spinnerets at the back of their abdomens. They perch on tall structures such as fence posts, stand on their tiptoes, raise their abdomens, and release the silk, creating a balloon, or parachute. When the wind catches them, they are launched, landing wherever the breeze takes them, sometimes miles away.

Walt Whitman wrote a beautiful poem about ballooning:

"A Noiseless Patient Spider"
A noiseless patient spider,
I mark'd where on a little promontory it stood isolated,

Mark'd how to explore the vacant vast surrounding,
It launched forth filament, filament, filament, out of itself,
Ever unreeling them, ever tirelessly speeding them.
And you O my soul where you stand,
Surrounded, detached, in measureless oceans of space,
Ceaselessly musing, venturing, throwing, seeking the spheres
    to connect them,
Till the bridge you will need be form'd, till the ductile anchor hold,
Till the gossamer thread you fling catch somewhere, O my soul

I asked Jerome Rovner, a spider expert and professor emeritus of biological sciences at Ohio University, about the sudden appearance of our sheet weavers and he said they'd been there all along. "With cooler temperatures in the morning in September than July, dew may be more likely to coat the silk of the webs," he said. As spiders age and mature, their webs become larger and may also be built higher in the vegetation, making it more likely for humans to take notice.

We also had a grass spider, or a "funnel weaver"—perhaps an *Agelenopsis pennsylvanica*—that had woven a funnel into my boxwood shrub. A flat section of the web extended across the top of the garden wall and through clematis prunings I'd neglected to remove—an extra clever trap, I thought. This spider hides inside the funnel and when it detects prey by vibration on the web, it races out to grab it—fast. I have stood and watched and seen only

fleetingly its brown body and hairy legs. There's a superstition about grass spiders: When there is dew on their webs in the lawn in the morning, it will be a beautiful day.

The black and yellow garden spider, an orbweaver of the family Araneidae, is easy to spot. It spins a spectacular zigzag in the middle of its web, called a stabilimentum. No one knows exactly why spiders create such decoration, though theories abound: as a decoy, to prevent birds from flying into the web, to use up extra silk, as thermoregulation, and others. The least likely explanation is to stabilize the web, even though that's how the stabilimentum got its name.

Another orbweaver is the barn spider, *Araneus cavaticus*, three-quarters of an inch long, which rebuilds its web nightly. We have an abundance of barn spiders in our barn and outbuildings on the farm. In his wonderful book *Charlotte's Web*, E.B. White used a barn spider as a prototype for Charlotte (her full name is Charlotte A. Cavatica) who tried to save the life of a pig by weaving words into her web.

I'd read that White tried to hatch some of his own barn spiders, so I decided to follow his lead and cut a few sacs from a web in our barn. I put the sacs into a box, punched holes in it, and brought it inside. But it was February, not October when White conducted his experiment, and my sacs were brown and shriveled, so I worried they were too old. I had no idea if they contained spiderlings.

I put the box by the kitchen window for a few days, but feared too much of a draft, so I moved it to a warmer spot. A week later, nothing had happened. I asked Dr. Rovner if he knew any tricks and he kindly gave me a few, including looking with a magnifying glass for exit holes, but in the end his best advice was to wait and see. I waited. I checked the box periodically. Nothing. But nine days later in the early morning I turned on the light over the stove, opened the box carefully, and saw inside, crawling around on a newly made dragline, a tiny brown dot with a grey abdomen. I sat down to write this and went back to look at the baby spider. I poured tea and went back to look at the baby spider. When my husband called, I told him with glee about our new resident, a baby spider.

Oh my soul.

ANIMALS

Porcupines

THIS IS HOW A PORCUPINE ATTACKS.

It turns its back and displays the black line edged with white running down the middle of its tail.

Its body shivers.

Its jaw clenches, incisors vibrate, and teeth clatter.

It emits an odor.

Quills become erect.

These are mere warnings.

If that's not enough to deter a predator, only then does the porcupine let loose its greatest defense: a quick flick of the tail that can release up to thirty thousand quills.

But the quills are not projectiles.

"It is probably this split-second tail slap that has given rise to the persistent but false rumor that porcupines throw their quills," Uldis Roze writes in *The North American Porcupine*.

I have never seen a porcupine. How do I know, then, that porcupines live nearby? That in spring, summer, and fall they sleep by day in trees, and in winter in rocky dens or one of our outbuildings, leaving at dusk, walking the earth only at night? Because I've seen porcupine quills embedded in the muzzles of a giant schnauzer and a golden retriever, confirmed with a night-time visit to a vet, where he, my husband, our daughter, and I removed three hundred quills from two sedated dogs. The dogs had stuck their snouts where they weren't welcome, presumably smack into the porcupine's neck.

"The predator's own momentum embeds the quills," Roze writes.

I know we have porcupines because I saw in last winter's dullness the base and snake-like roots of an elm gnawed by a porcupine in a triangular pattern that shone a vibrant cinnamon against an otherwise gray landscape.

"The pattern of tooth scrapes left on the bark by an adult porcupine displays the animal's craftsmanship," Roze writes. Like beavers, porcupines use orange incisors to chew down to the cambium, but Roze describes the porcupine's gnawing as more finely finished than the beaver, the bark removed in "five or six scrapes converging on an apex, like sticks in a tepee."

John Wenzel, director of Powdermill Nature Reserve, has seen porcupines. "This is a huge year for them," he said. "I don't know why." Usually, he sees a porcupine once every two years, but this year he'd seen five by August, and others have reported seeing porcupine roadkill.

Wenzel showed me what he described as "terrible, wonderful damage" that has killed big trees on Powdermill's Porcupine Ridge trail. At seventeen hundred feet, the trail was named for three tulip poplars girdled by porcupines. The fifty-year-old trees remain standing for visitors to see (unlike beavers, porcupines do not fell trees) but none will survive long. When I told Wenzel I wanted to see niptwigs, little did I know what a journey he'd take me on: a harrowing ride in an all-terrain vehicle deeper into Powdermill's woods, on rocky trails, through thick brush, up and down riverbanks, and over fallen trees.

Niptwigs he showed me: the remains of twigs chewed at an angle, tossed by porcupines from atop a hemlock. Porcupines eat small twigs and needles of the hemlock, but not the bark because of the high tannin content. Piles of niptwigs rested on the forest floor.

I've not seen porcupines shimmy up and down trees, aided as they are by textured footpads, tail bristles that prevent back-sliding, and curved claws for grabbing. Nor have I seen them fall out of trees, which they do fairly often, reaching a tad too far for a tasty morsel. About one-third of porcupine skeletons reveal multiple broken bones, some of which don't heal properly and then prevent them from climbing—hence nibbling a tree's base instead of the preferred crown.

Weighing twelve to thirty-five pounds, the North

American porcupine (*Erethizon dorsatum*) is the largest of the New World's porcupines (and North America's second largest rodent after the beaver), but they lack the advantage of their South American cousins: a prehensile tail. Weight helps them survive the cold but can result in mighty hard falls. Sometimes they even impale themselves on their own quills.

Tumbles notwithstanding, porcupines generally live five to seven years—although Roze followed one that lived until twenty-one. They measure about eighteen inches in length, with an additional eight inches for the tail. Porcupines head into dens in November, but do not hibernate. Forty percent of their body weight is lost during winter.

Those who do see porcupines up close can't help but notice the parasites that live on them. "Hands down they are the most heavily parasitized mammal in North America," said Stephen Rogers, Collection Manager of Section of Birds at Pittsburgh's Carnegie Museum of Natural History who wrote his master's thesis on porcupines. Porcupines have tapeworms and roundworms, ticks, fleas, lice, and occasionally scabies, a mite that burrows into skin, makes the hair fall out, and can cause death.

Porcupines are herbivores, eating a diet of leaves, fruit, buds, nuts, and bark, none of which supplies adequate salt, so the animal voraciously seeks out the mineral. "They'll eat ax handles," Rogers said. "I have seen them chew on natural gas pumping stations out in the woods of northern Pennsylvania, and they love chewing aluminum signs because the aluminum corrodes and forms a salt." Porcupines munch on plants covered in road salt and particularly like plywood—bringing them too close to cars and people, which can be lethal.

Mating, which occurs in the fall, is not as spiky as one might imagine. The female curls her tail upward to expose the quill-free underside; the male places his forepaws on the back, or stands erect. The seven-month gestation is "one of the longest known in the animal world," Roze writes. A single, one-pound baby is born, with fur and quills inside an amniotic sac. The quills are soft until the mother licks off the sac, then harden within an hour.

I so enjoyed Uldis Roze's book that I called to ask if he'd speak to me. Professor emeritus from Queens College at CUNY, Roze is perhaps the world's preeminent expert on North American porcupines. He was as gracious as his book is fascinating. We spoke first of the fisher, the porcupine's fiercest natural predator, which repeatedly attacks the porcupine's quill-free face until it becomes disoriented and cannot turn backward. "Fishers are an efficient hunter of baby porcupines," he said. Reintroduced in New York State in the 1970s and in Pennsylvania in the 1980s, fishers have reduced porcupine populations by 90 percent or more, Roze told me. "Our population has sunk, bottomed out," he said from his home in the Catskills. "Porcupines do best where fishers are least."

He kindly answered a slew of my questions.

Baby porcupines aren't really called porcupettes?

They are.

What is a station tree?

A "rest tree" where they sleep during the day.

And a witch tree?

A tree with a disoriented canopy caused by years of feeding on the upper bark. It can look like a broom or other shapes, but always stands out, looks unnatural, and often has porcupine droppings on the ground below. The porcupine itself is seldom seen in the witch tree because it feeds at night.

What does the porcupine smell like?

Like nothing else in the forest. (His writings include the words invasive, powerful, pungent, and repellent.) *"One's eyes begin to water and the nose runs."*

Are quills hollow or is that a myth?

Quills are not hollow, but have a spongy matrix in the middle, which doesn't add weight, but adds rigidity. The quills have surface fatty acids that kill bacteria and act as an antibiotic. If you get a wood splinter, it can swell and become infected; a porcupine quill won't do that.

Some have referred to the porcupine as unkempt.

The quills are straight and clean. A relaxed porcupine looks as neatly combed as a model for hair lotion.

Should quills be cut to remove them?

No. Pull them out. Since they are barbed like fishhooks, be careful not to lose your grip or the tip can travel deeper into the skin.

Do males urinate on females before mating?

They do, but in drops, not a stream. It's not a water sport but brings the female into estrus.

Do females really spend nearly their entire lives pregnant?

Seven months pregnant, four nursing, and one for mating. Repeat.

Have porcupines been affected by climate change?

They may have benefitted because the species has expanded north into the Aleutian peninsula of Alaska where they were absent previously.

How did niptwigs get its name?

Niptwig is a word I made up and it is now accepted by Scrabble.

How might I find a porcupine?

Fall and winter are the best seasons to see porcupines. Summer, forget it. You'll never see a porcupine in a tree with leaves on it. Look up into leafless tree canopies for a black mass against the sky. Follow tracks in the snow to dens, such as rock outcroppings or crevices with urine at the entrance. Take a flashlight and look inside.

Roze is a man who has seen porcupines, tracked them, studied them, held them. But for me, the porcupine remains elusive. I was reticent at first writing about an animal I had not seen, but then so much of the natural world *is* just beyond our sight, creating a kind of blind faith that allows our imaginations to take over. And isn't that part of the wonder of it all: the nighttime sound of the Great Horned Owl; the smell of a skunk; cracked walnut shells lined up on a stone wall, presumably by chipmunks. We may not see such creatures, but we know they are here, living among us.

And what a joy to search for the porcupine, to look up into leafless trees. Examine potential dens. Forage for niptwigs under our farm's hemlocks. Keep my eye out for witch trees and try to identify the animal's scent. I know now to listen for cries between competing males, and in winter, I will hunt for the porcupine's distinctive tracks in the snow, wide tails sweeping behind.

Beavers

IN MY SMALL AND RANDOM SURVEY, PEOPLE KNOW THAT BEAVERS CHEW
wood, build dams, have big teeth and large tails. That's about all I knew, until
beavers moved into our farm pond. Turns out there are many interesting facts
to learn about North America's largest rodent, *Castor canadensis*.

The basics are that beavers are three to four feet long, weigh up to seventy
pounds, and have fur ranging from blonde to charcoal. Propelled by webbed
hind feet, they can swim up to six miles per hour and stay underwater for
fifteen minutes. They're herbivores, semiaquatic, mostly nocturnal, live in
family-oriented colonies, and are territorial. Even more interesting, their teeth
are orange—due to the enamel's iron content—self-sharpen, grow continually,
and if not aligned properly, can prevent beavers from gnawing, grow too long,
and cause a beaver to starve to death. In autumn, beavers drag tree branches to
the bottom of a pond and stick them into mud, creating a winter larder. Skin
flaps behind their teeth allow them to haul those branches without swallowing
water, and beavers have a translucent third eyelid so they can see underwater,
as well as valves on their ears and a nose that shuts when submerged.

The sound of running water drives them crazy. They think their dam has
sprung a leak and run to patch it. "They're like the Army Corps of Engineers,"
said Dr. Thorvald Holmes, a retired biologist at Humboldt State University in
California. "If they stop the sound of water, they'll create a pond and they're
in business. If they don't pay attention to running water, it reduces the likeli-
hood of being a successful beaver." Beavers have an outer fur and an under fur,
which Holmes said acts as a wet suit. Air gets trapped between these layers,
and if they don't dive deep, their bodies never get wet. Native Americans
called the beaver "the sacred center of the earth" because their dam building
creates a habitat for so many creatures.

"Grooming is also a big deal for a beaver," Holmes said, "because if you
undermine that under fur, if it gets greasy or sticky, it loses its insulating properties." He said the easiest task to see a beaver do is preen (the hind feet have
special preening toes) "and tease their hair to make sure they have loft in their

under fur." Beavers' scaly tails are amazing: they slap them against the water to warn of danger, balance on them to stand upright, and use them as a rudder when swimming. Fat is stored in the tail for winter, and it regulates body temperature. Trappers were known to roast the fatty appendage on an open fire.

Beaver can be eaten during Lent since the Catholic Church declared in the seventeenth century that because beavers spend so much time in the water, they could be considered a fish. Bootleggin' BBQ in St. Louis, Missouri, put beaver on their Lenten menu in 2016, marinating it with brown sugar and grilling it, serving it with mashed potatoes, and making it into tacos or boudin balls. Brenton Brown, partner and pitmaster, wore a t-shirt during Lent printed with the words "God said it was Ok." In other non-scientific realms, the beaver is an official emblem of Canada, featured opposite Queen Elizabeth on the Canadian nickel, because, according to the *Canadian Dictionary*, beavers are noted for their "industry, skill, and perseverance, qualities considered suitable for a nation to emulate."

Between 60 and 400 million beavers lived in North America before European settlers arrived and nearly wiped them out. "The single most important species in the fur trade was the beaver," Holmes said. (In 1903, Pennsylvania reintroduced and protected beavers.) The beaver's outer fur was used for coats, but the under fur, which Holmes described as "velvety, glossy, and luxurious" was most coveted and pressed into felt for fancy hats, including top hats. Beavers were also trapped for castoreum, used in perfume (castoreum hold its scent a long time, Holmes said), in medicine, and as a food additive. Castoreum comes from one of the anal glands near the beaver's tail, secretions from which the beaver uses to mark territory and rub on their fur to repel water.

My husband first noticed beaver activity at the farm when mowing the field around the pond. The weeping willows he'd planted had been felled, as well as cherry and ash trees, the recognizable *V* shape typical of beaver activity. Beavers like willow because it's easy to peel; willow also contains salicylic acid, the same ingredient as aspirin. "The willow cure," Holmes joked, "they don't get headaches." Beavers strip tree bark by turning the branch like an ear of corn, trying to reach the cambium, a sweet, nutritious layer between the bark and wood. They also eat aquatic plants such as cattails and water lilies, both of which we have in abundance at our pond.

Around the pond's perimeter, we noticed multiple lodges built of sticks and mud, but what we couldn't see below were separate rooms for giving birth, sleeping, and eating, an underwater entrance, or an air vent, common in beaver lodges. Most lodges contain a single family of two to twelve, including a breeding pair, kits, and yearlings. Yearlings generally help raise the newborns and stay with their parents until around age two, then venture off on their own. Beavers often mate for life, and breeding season is January through March, gestation about three months, and average litter size is three to five kits. Babies swim within a half hour of birth and while beavers don't hibernate, they mostly stay inside the lodge during winter.

Beavers are touted for being nature's engineers, creating habitats for animals such as moose, deer, fish, waterfowl, otters, mink, songbirds, frogs, and others. "If humans are the world's most influential mammals, beavers have a fair claim at second place," wrote Ben Goldfarb in *Eager: The Surprising, Secret Life of Beavers and Why they Matter*. In his book, Goldfarb asks his readers to appreciate the many benefits beavers bring to the environment. "Beavers are environmental Swiss Army knives, capable of tackling just about any ecological dilemma," he writes. "Trying to slow down floods or filter out pollution? There's a beaver for that. Hoping to capture more water for agriculture in the face of climate change? Add a beaver. Concerned about erosion, salmon runs, or wildfire? Take two beaver families and check back in a year."

But what does one do when beavers build a dam on a spillway, which could cause a pond to breach its bank? Or protect the trees? We put wire around the small trees that remained and then beavers began to gnaw on a big weeping willow, a tree we didn't want to lose. So, I called Samara Trusso, wildlife manager with the Pennsylvania Game Commission, SW region, who said the Game Commission is "hands off when it comes to beavers unless we have complaints." Of course, they do get complaints—666 in PA in 2016—from farmers, business owners, and PennDot—plugged culverts, flooded roads, and downed nursery trees. "They can be a challenging species," she said.

Depending on the complaint, the Game Commission may connect homeowners with a licensed trapper, who can trap beavers legally from December

26 to March 30. In Westmoreland County where we live, the bag limit is twenty per season. But since the price for pelts has gone down from $33 per pelt in 1987 to $8.81 today, there are fewer trappers (from 2,475 in 2007 to 2,131 now), and consequently fewer trapped beavers—from 8,408 in 2000 to 7,417 in 2017. Still, Pennsylvania doled out 43,329 "furbearer" licenses in 2017, so a few people must be in the woods hunting beaver, raccoon, skunk, opossum, bobcat, porcupine, and others.

Beavers can be relocated, Trusso said, but that's time and labor intensive and stressful for the beavers. And "if you don't take the entire colony, you haven't solved the problem." Adult beavers will travel dozens of miles to get back to their original territory, she said. Relocating juveniles is easier.

Neither trapping nor relocating were activities I relished; I preferred to live in harmony with beavers. So, I suggested to John Wenzel of Powdermill that we record their activity, hoping some footage of local beavers might be an interesting feature at the Nimick Nature Center down the road. We met at our pond, along with James and Max, who brought cameras and a "GoPro," and set up for time-lapse and nighttime photography. But after weeks of checking the cameras, we got no footage. What did we do wrong? Holmes said we "came into their environment and created a disturbance. They didn't like it." We should have left the cameras for an extended amount of time without checking them, he said, "wasted some film, burned up some batteries" so the beavers got used to seeing the gear.

To observe the beavers, Holmes said to go to the pond at dawn without a light, be quiet, and sit behind a barrier. "Hang out and let the animal do what it would normally do without disturbing it." But I had already done that. One foggy morning I ventured out around dawn, set up camp under the big willow, a cup of tea to warm me. Fish jumped. I heard the call of a kingfisher. I was quiet. I waited. No beavers. Still, there are few more peaceful ways to start one's day than sitting by a pond in the early morning looking for beavers.

I'll be back, but in the meantime, I'll contemplate this ecological comment from Holmes: "The only hope we have is for *Homo sapiens*, a species leagues ahead of beavers in their ability to change their habitats, to begin to think about our planet, and consider whether it is of any value to us. Failing that, we are toast." I will also consider questions posed to me by my friend Susan, who studies shamanism and gave me the book *Animal Speak: The Spiritual and Magic Powers of Creatures Great and Small*, by Ted Andrews. "If a beaver has come into your life, ask yourself some important questions," he wrote. "Have you been neglecting your most basic dreams? Are your dreams in need of repair? Remember that the beaver reminds us we have to act on our dreams to make them a reality."

A Horse

THERE HAVE BEEN PHONE CALLS IN MY LIFE I WISH I'D NEVER RECEIVED. I was cold and wet from swimming in an Irish lake when I returned to the house to see my husband standing in the driveway. Waiting for me. That wasn't normal. My father had called. My mother was dead. She was unloading the dishwasher when an aneurism burst.

One night after my plane landed in Florida and taxied to the terminal, I opened my cell phone and heard a message from my husband. Our son had had a bad accident. "Not life threatening, but not good," he said.

Last winter at dusk I was just slipping my feet into my muck boots to go close the chicken coop when my cell phone rang. It was Dave, who helps with our horse. "Hershey has fallen on the ice," he told me.

I'd worried about a horse falling on ice on our driveway for thirty years. To get from barn to pasture and back again, horse and leader must traverse blacktop, which can be treacherous in winter. On icy spots, we sprinkle sand or wood ash and lead the horses out the back door of the barn where there's more grass and less blacktop, but still, blacktop is unavoidable. We've tried to change the path, but the configuration of our property—barn, house, stream, bridge, driveway, and lawn—makes it impossible. Winter poses another problem: ice and snow accumulate under Hershey's hooves while he's in the pasture, and unless we lift each of his legs and knock the ice off with a mallet before bringing him inside, he might as well be skating down the driveway with icy tennis balls on his horseshoes.

I found Dave and our eighteen-hundred-pound Clydesdale/Thoroughbred cross on the ground in the middle of the driveway. Dave's girlfriend's horse, Frankie, was loose and needed to be taken to the barn, so I grabbed him and walked as gingerly as I could. On icy days I worry about myself too—or whomever is holding the lead rope. If a horse falls on the ice, the human is likely going with him. (Dave was lucky that night; he stumbled and his feet slid out from under him, but he caught his balance.) I put Frankie into his stall and our two dogs in another so they wouldn't be underfoot. I went back to Dave, still on the ground with Hershey.

"Hi, my Hersh," I said softly, the same nickname and tone I always use. "Hi, my Hersh Hersh." When he heard my voice, he looked up at me and made a valiant effort to stand, legs flying and body writhing, but he couldn't. He lay there and moaned.

"I think it's his right rear ankle," Dave said.

Dave and I were the only two on the farm that night and the least knowledgeable horse people. But I did know that horses can't stay on the ground long. "When a horse goes down, time is of the essence," Connie, our vet, had said. We needed help and we needed it fast.

Connie had just had a baby and wasn't on call, but her office said they'd send Anita, another vet, and Kami, the vet tech, as soon as possible. I called our friend, John, an excavator by trade and an Irish horse-whisperer of sorts, who, by the grace of some higher being, had just returned from South Carolina at three o'clock that morning. He said he'd be right over. He suggested I call another fellow, Kevin, for an extra pair of hands.

I tease my husband that he's never at the farm when the real disasters occur, but that's not fair. He's been home for his share of fires, floods, and dying dogs, but the day Hershey went down, he was at a board meeting at a local university forty minutes away. I didn't know exactly where or with whom he was meeting, and I knew he'd have his cell phone turned off, so I called the campus police. A kind woman answered, I explained the situation to her, and to my surprise, she said her daughter had been in pony club with our daughter. She'd try to find my husband.

Hershey is a big-boned, gentle giant of a gelding, dark brown and black, with a white blaze on his nose. Three out of four of his furry feet are white. The fourth is black. About twenty-seven years old, he came to us nineteen years ago from Virginia, where my husband had ridden him, liked him, and bought him. Hershey was head-shy when he first arrived, abused in some way we figured, but in no short time I taught him to give me horse kisses when I offered carrots. "Kisses," I'd say, and he always complied. Sometimes he nearly knocked my teeth out, but I still found joy when his big muzzle came my way. His eyes are a deep penetrating black, his tail thick, wide, and long, and he's a character. He leans out of his stall to nuzzle with the dogs, and in summer positions his head toward the fan, his black forelock sweeping backward so he looks like Elvis Presley. He's one of the few horses that ever made me feel comfortable on his back.

I am the family member who came late to horseback riding, beginning lessons when I was forty with our son, then five. He and I took lessons together

in Ireland in a small, sloppy, and crowded riding ring, head to tail with a slew of other nags, nearly always in the rain. (If you don't ride in the rain in Ireland, you don't ride.) The conditions weren't ideal, but our teacher was good, and we learned a lot. Eventually I jumped three feet and galloped across our fields, but I never got completely over my fear. My husband, on the other hand, has ridden his entire life, and our daughter was foxhunting at four on a pony on a lead-line behind him, flying over jumps, begging to go faster and higher. She came home afterward to drink milk out of a baby bottle. Over many years in pony club, she rode two fiery ponies—and Hershey.

Dave and I waited in the near dark with light only from our cell phones. Dave's battery was running low. I must have gotten a flashlight, though I don't remember doing so. The temperature was frigid. Dave didn't have gloves on, but he wouldn't let me relieve him. He insisted on staying on the ground next to Hershey, trying to calm him. I paced and kneeled down to rub Hershey's neck. "It's alright, Hersh," I said. Over and over. Hershey kept trying to get up, but he couldn't. He continued to moan. We heard Frankie whinnying in the barn, annoyed at being left alone. There was no visible moon or stars. When I looked up toward the heavens that night it was only to say a silent prayer to save our horse.

I could see it all play out in my head. Hershey had broken a bone. Help would arrive, but the only option would be to put him down. Lethal drugs would come out of the vet's truck and Hershey would be given a shot. I'd have to stand there and watch him die. I'd be a mess but would try and hold it together. After the medicine took effect, we'd pick up Hershey in the tractor bucket and set him at a burial site. It would all happen too fast and not fast enough.

That wasn't just my grim imagination. John told me later that his first thought when I called him was: "I am going to go meet a vet and dig a hole."

Our large, white and green nineteenth-century barn was not used for horses by the previous owner, but when we bought the farm thirty years ago, my husband said, "animals bring the fields alive." How right he was. We built stalls, a turnout shed, and fixed up a smaller barn for cows. We've had five belted Galloways (Oh *you* have the oreo cows, strangers always said to me), and a motley crew of goats, sheep, ducks, chickens, geese, turkeys, rabbits, dogs, a donkey, barn and house cats, horses, and ponies. Hershey is our last large animal, and I couldn't imagine our farm without him.

But if we couldn't get Hershey to stand, he could be dead in a matter of hours. His massive weight compressed his lungs, heart, and muscle tissue, so eventually he'd struggle to pump blood to his extremities, which could result in "compartment syndrome" where muscle tissue dies from lack of blood. His size was not to his advantage; ponies can stay down longer because they weigh less, Connie told me, but all horses "need to get up, roll around, shake, and then they can go back down," she said.

Hershey couldn't get up for two reasons. One, his legs pointed uphill so he couldn't get his legs underneath him to stand. Imagine falling on the ski slope and your feet are uphill. Secondly, he couldn't get any traction on the ice.

Headlights came down the driveway. Dave's girlfriend, Elle, was first. She parked her car up high as a signal to others to stop and in order not to spook Hershey. She sprinkled ash around Hershey to offer traction, and brought food and water, "to give him some energy, rehydrate if he's tired," she said. Hershey ate some grain out of her hand but couldn't eat out of a bucket. John came next, then Anita and Kami—both of whom had also been in pony club with our daughter. Kevin arrived, now seven of us in all.

I sensed John had ideas about how to handle the situation, but he deferred to the vet. Anita examined Hershey's legs and pelvis and felt his pulses. She didn't think anything was broken, but she couldn't be sure about the leg he was lying on. John watched Anita and noticed that Hershey was able to help her, a good sign that his legs still had strength to move. John examined Hershey. "I asked all his legs to move, and they did," he said. His conclusion was also that no bones were broken—but neither was positive.

My husband called in the middle of all this, and I explained what was happening. A woman had located him in the board meeting and said the police were looking for him. I imagined his eyes widening. She told him there was a horse problem at home. He left the meeting and headed to the farm.

John had a plan. We'd move Hershey by attaching one end of a strap to Hershey's front leg and the other end to the front bumper of Kevin's pick-up truck—a risky strategy that could harm Hershey more. "We had a better chance of things going wrong than right," John said. But his rationale was this: "Where are we now? We're at zero. If we're at zero, anything I try, even if it fails, I am still only at zero. Nothing is worse than zero." The vet, he said, had one tool in her toolbox: a syringe. And no one wanted to use that.

It could be dangerous for us too. Horses panic when they feel trapped, their fight or flight mechanism kicks in, and they flail and kick. (Anita and Kami, I found out later, were pregnant at the time.) To prevent injuries, John asked that we follow his direction only, that no one else shout out commands. I remember thinking I might scream or cry, but I certainly wasn't yelling out any commands. We complied, were quiet, watched, and waited.

The strap was attached to Hershey's front leg and to Kevin's truck. Kevin got behind the steering wheel. John asked Dave to move from his perch next to Hershey's head, but Dave didn't budge. John insisted, I backed him up, and finally Dave agreed. I sensed that Dave felt Hershey's fall was his responsibility and wanted to stay close.

Kevin backed up the truck. "Just go easy," John said. John used hand signals to guide him. Slowly, Kevin dragged Hershey off the tarmac. We were fortunate Hershey had a blanket on, which helped him slide, prevented shaving off hair, and kept him warm if he went into shock. We were lucky Hershey was a warmblood, not a thoroughbred. "A thoroughbred would commit suicide before he'd let us help him," John said. "They hit the panic button, and everything goes wrong." But Hershey was compliant and allowed us to do whatever we could to help him.

"Hershey spun like a helicopter," John said.

Hershey now lay on a thin sliver of grass next to a stream in a better position, his head above his legs. But his feet still needed to be flipped over so he'd have some traction on grass instead of tarmac.

John's next idea was to attach the strap to one of Hershey's back legs and flip him. He asked the other two men to get on the same side of the horse with him. "We were in the most dangerous place in the world," John said, with a horse's legs spinning toward them and not much room to move. "If Hershey jumped up, staggered and fell, he was falling on top of us." John gave the men an escape plan—where to run after the flip to avoid getting hurt.

The strap was attached, and the three men lined up. I heard what I thought was a gunshot. I jumped. But it wasn't a gunshot. John had whacked Hershey's flank with the other end of the strap, which hit the horse blanket and made a thunderous sound. Hershey's legs flipped. The men ran out of the way. Hershey bolted upright, and stood on all fours.

Seven of us exhaled at the same time.

"I needed to make Hershey think it *was* a shotgun going off," John said. "He needed to use every sense he had in his mind and body to leave town." It was a split-second decision. "You only get one chance to scare the bejesus out of him," he said.

Horses, Anita explained, want to run away "from pain and scariness and noises and such." John got Hershey right at the right angle, she said. "He got him moving, that's for sure."

We walked Hershey back and forth across the grass so Anita and John could assess his condition. They concluded he was stiff, but sound. Anita gave him a painkiller and an anti-inflammatory in case he was sore. We brought Frankie back out from his stall and put both horses in the pasture for the night. Anita and John agreed that Hershey should stay out of the stall for the night and keep moving so his muscles didn't freeze up.

"I've never had a situation turn out so well," Kami said.

"Hershey's a legend," Anita said. He had long been one of the most popular horses in pony club, and that night he showed his mettle again. "He has a good head on his shoulders."

I walked over to John and threw my arms around his neck, a bit too bold perhaps as I didn't know him that well. But I was so grateful. I thanked everyone who came out of their warm houses and offices on a freezing night to save the life of a horse.

Hershey was skittish for a couple days. He didn't want to come into the barn or walk on the driveway again. When Anita came back the next day to check on him, Hershey wouldn't come to us, even though we had a bucket of feed. He ran the other direction—proof enough he was truly alright.

"Really, honest to goodness, it was pure luck that my attempt worked," John said. He gave the rest of us credit for making the night successful: for keeping Hershey relaxed, for staying focused, for having a vet there, which gave him comfort. "It was good to get a licensed second opinion," he said.

A team effort, John called it, and a huge achievement. But I know differently. There's no doubt in my mind that without John we would have lost our beloved horse.

Animal Tracking

FROM PHOTOGRAPHS I SENT TO EXPERT TRACKER LINDA SPIELMAN, SHE WAS able to tell me wonderful little stories about what animals on our farm were doing last winter. At the top of the hill, a mouse bounded across deep snow, its hind feet sinking into holes made by its front feet. "Lots of animals do this kind of thing in deep snow because it takes less energy than making new holes with the hind feet," she said. "Imagine walking behind someone in a foot of snow. You would probably step in the holes made by the person you were following."

In the woods, a squirrel paused on all four feet, then stood up on its hind legs—scared perhaps, or maybe just looking around. It made a small leap and took off again.

In the field where we gallop our horses, a vole made a tunnel on top of a hard layer of snow and under a lighter layer.

"We were all trackers once," Spielman writes in her book *A Field Guide to Tracking Mammals in the Northeast*, referring to our hunter-gatherer ancestors who tracked for food for survival. But when that became unnecessary, tracking was nearly a lost art. Now, thanks to field biologists, conservationists, wildlife officials, ecologists, and amateur naturalists, tracking has been resurrected. "It is more acceptable now as a reasonable tool to study wildlife," she said. Tracking schools can be found throughout the country; Spielman teaches tracking classes in Ithaca, New York.

I am not an expert tracker, only an amateur observer, but I like tracking because I want to know which creatures live among us—those we can see, and those we cannot. So, last winter, after a lovely snowfall, I went into the forest, camera in hand, to see what tracks I could discover.

Finding tracks was the easy part. Identifying them was not. Coyote tracks can look like dogs; rabbits like bobcats; mink like squirrels; small, hopping birds like mice. Spielman admitted that tracking is "a lifetime journey," but said, "Don't be intimidated and say you don't know enough. Just get out there and look!"

Still, do not do as I did. Be prepared.

I should have taken with me six basic items: a camera, a notebook, a pencil, a six-inch clear ruler, a tracking guide, and measuring tape—because measuring, I learned, is key to proper identification. I should have measured the length and width of the footprint itself and the distance between footprints, because that reveals the speed and gait at which the animal was moving. Spielman recognizes five basic gaits: walk, trot, bound, lope, and gallop. I should have measured the width of the overall track pattern too because if I'm confused, say, whether a track is a chipmunk or a red squirrel, I need to know that chipmunk trails are usually 2⅛ to 3⅛ inches wide, whereas red squirrels are 3 to 4½ inches.

A zigzag is the most common track pattern, Spielman said, which indicates a walking gait—right, then left, then right, similar to the way we walk, and includes such animals as cats, dogs, deer, and bear. A straight-line pattern, on the other hand, indicates animals that bound, like rabbits and squirrels. Their tracks show all four feet together, then a space, then four more feet.

Trackers say it's often easier to get a good measurement of a track pattern than the track itself because footprints look different depending on the ground being walked upon: snow, mud, sand, or clay—called substrate in tracker lingo. "Substrate adds an extra complication to tracking," Spielman said. Other complications include animals that spread their toes in different ways, aging tracks that get rained on or covered in new snow, and animals that have more hair on their feet in winter so their tracks look different. I was fooled initially by snow that had fallen from trees and made marks on the ground. "Snow plops!" Spielman said immediately, giving them a name, "another thing that can cause confusion."

To help identify animals, Spielman said to look for other signs as well: scat, urine, nibbled shrubs, felled trees, dens, and middens—or refuse heaps— powerful clues to which animals are about. Chewed acorns might indicate the presence of gray squirrels, black pellets that white-tailed deer have been near, and gnawing at the base of a tree the work of a porcupine.

Know which animals live in your region, she advised, and use all your senses. Listen for the bark of a mother fox alerting her young. Know that red fox urine smells like skunk. Touch the tooth grooves on trees felled by beavers and feel the iciness of a winter deer bed. Spielman even encourages her students to taste sap in late winter and early spring when squirrels make the sap run by biting the branches of sugar maples.

Tracking is more than a good way to know where animals roam; it's a visual language that tells us when animals are scared, who's chasing them, and what they eat. That's where the stories come in. "All of a sudden, there's a little scene going on, a clue to what animal it is, but also to what happened," Spielman explained. Radio collars, she said, can tell us an animal's location, but tracking tells us "what they did all day, every day, for days and days, and gives you all kinds of other information."

Paul Rezendes, tracker and wildlife photographer, writes in his book *Tracking and the Art of Seeing*: "Tracking an animal makes us sensitive to it—a bond is formed, an intimacy develops. We begin to realize that what is happening to the animals and to the planet is actually happening to us. We are all one."

If we are all one, might tracking encourage us to protect the wildlife in our own backyards, to help conserve their habitats? Spielman thinks so. "If people don't know the animals that live around them, they won't care." Tracking, she said, makes the lives of animals real—as real as our neighbors next door. "And if we don't care about them, we human beings can do real damage."

What if future trackers tracked us? What sort of footprint will we leave that might be discovered; what might our tracks suggest? What "little story" will our movements tell about our short time on this fragile planet we call earth?

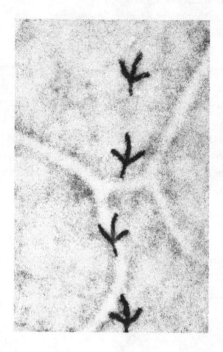

HOUSE
AND
GARDEN

My Vegetable Garden in Springtime

I came to love my rows, my beans . . . they attached me to the earth, and so I got strength, like Antaeus.

—HENRY DAVID THOREAU, *WALDEN*

MY FAVORITE TIME IN THE VEGETABLE GARDEN IS IN SPRING, AFTER THE soil is tilled and before the seeds are planted. Perennials are poking up—chervil, lovage, sorrel—but otherwise there's little growth, just a blank canvas. The weather is cool, less humid and with fewer bugs, and it is a joy to dig in the dirt after a long winter. I love to feel the soil between my fingers, the sun on my face, and as I survey the dark earth in geometric rows, the scene is orderly and full of promise, or, as Samuel Johnson said, "the triumph of hope over experience."

I imagine rows of cabbage uneaten by white moths. Eggplant without aphids. Tomatoes with no blight. Cucumbers without beetles. Broccoli with no worms. Raspberry canes artfully wound around wire, and strawberries tucked in with straw. Enough rain and no nibbling creatures—just healthy plants thriving without chemicals, all beautifully designed.

The bones of my garden, inspired long ago by a visit to Williamsburg, Virginia, consist of four, locust-lined quadrants, joined in the center by a stone circle of orange, red, and white poppies. In the middle of each quadrant is a white tuteur where I train morning glories, runner beans, and sweet peas. Above the quadrants are eight raised beds, and above that, a long row of raspberries. Below are asparagus and strawberry beds, and below that still, three beds for melons and pumpkins so vines can meander through the white pickets. Mulched paths, dotted with ceramic pots of agapanthus, dahlias, and *fraises des bois* run throughout.

But each spring within that basic pattern, I redesign, which is, for me, one of life's great pleasures. Which rows should be horizontal? Vertical? Where shall I place this year's cucumber trellis? Should I plant celery in a circle as my book advises? I contemplate crop rotation and companion planting and choose which volunteers to keep and where—borage, sunflowers, hollyhock, pansies, and nicotiana—for as much as I like order, I adore the whimsy of volunteers.

I decide where to plant zinnias, nasturtium, cosmos, and other flowers to attract bees and amend the soil with horse and chicken manure, compost, wood ash, and coffee grounds my husband kindly brings me by the bagful. I take out the green cloches and row covers to protect tender new plants, wade through mud, and tackle weeds I should have pulled last fall. Occasionally, though, I stop and raise my head, stand still for a moment, look around at the fluorescent green of the budding trees, and listen for the sweet sound of returning songbirds.

I have tended a western Pennsylvania garden for thirty-two years. At first, I did everything wrong, hardly knew the habit of a Jerusalem artichoke from a turnip. I ordered so many packets of arugula that the seed company called and asked if I were a business. I thought I needed to plant the entire garden on Memorial Day weekend—our first frost-free date—so I planted from dawn until dusk for three days. I didn't understand that cold-hardy vegetables such as spinach and radishes could be started as soon as the ground can be worked; peas, some say, on St. Patrick's Day. I did not know what our babysitter told me—that the last snowfall of the year is called onion snow, which is when onions should be planted. I knew nothing of succession planting, nor did I realize garlic was ideally planted the autumn before. And yet that first year was the only year, despite repeated attempts, that I grew small, round, orange-fleshed Charentais melons, as sweet and delectable as I imagine they are in France.

My lofty dreams begin to take shape each winter, long before the first buds of spring, as I ponder seed catalogues by the fire. Maybe this year, I will try rutabaga, speckled trout-back lettuce, snapdragons, or cardoons. The great British gardener

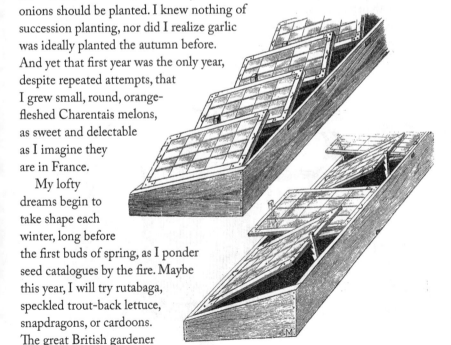

and poet Vita Sackville-West, whose Sissinghurst Castle Garden draws two hundred thousand visitors a year, must have studied catalogues similarly, as she wrote in her poem "Winter":

> *The Gardener sees what he will never see*
> *Here, in his lamp-lit parable, he'll scan*
> *Catalogues bright with colour and with hope, Dearest delusions*
>   *of creative mind.*

When my seeds arrive, I separate them into categories such as brassicas, herbs, or root vegetables, and plant them under grow lights in the barn, in wooden trays with wooden markers. I'm a purist here, avoiding plastic as best I can, aesthetics almost as important to me as seed growth. But then reality seeps in. Bugs come out of nowhere, mice shimmy up my seed-starting stand. I water too much or too little. I speak to the tender seedlings, occasionally even caress the leaves, but hard as I try to nurture them, some just wither and die.

Those that survive must get their true leaves, so while I wait, I line up in alphabetical order last year's plant markers, rewriting in black the words that faded in sun and rain. I gather up binder twine from hay bales to use as string, and, with help, jury-rig rotting trellises and raised beds so they will last yet another year. I walk in the woods and collect sticks to use as row markers. I like to recycle and reuse.

But in gardening, as in life, there is always room for improvement, and over the years I've grown to recognize my many gardening shortfalls. For one, I'm perhaps *too* thrifty, reusing pots and potting soil when I should use new. I am heavy-handed when transplanting seedlings, vowing each year to be more delicate. I am impatient, wishing plants to harden off faster than necessary, and I can be greedy, planting seedlings too close together as if that will produce more when the opposite is true. And by some trick of nature, if I plant five squash seeds to thin to two as the packet instructs, the two strongest always end up right next to each other, revealing another serious flaw of mine: I hate to thin. Never can I justify plucking heartlessly out of the soil a perfectly healthy plant that has worked equally as hard to germinate and grow. Lettuce thinnings I eat, of course, but the same cannot be said of a zucchini plant. I always feel guilty.

I am so bothered by the question of thinning that I consult an expert. Do plants feel pain? I ask Simon Gilroy, professor of botany at the University of Wisconsin, whose lab specializes in how plants respond to environmental cues, such as thinning. "Yes, they do sense that they are being wounded and start up antiherbivore defenses," he said, "but that is a very different thing from something like our feeling of pain which is both sensation and emotion layered on each other. I think you are completely right to appreciate plants for the amazing pieces of biology that they are, but I would not lose sleep over your gardening."

Nevertheless, I try to give the thinned plants away.

Years ago, when I lived and worked in New York City, I escaped to my parents' house in Connecticut, where my mother and I gardened together. "Dirt Therapy," we called it, but we hardly invented the concept of gardening as healing, which has long been well documented: time slows down, we meditate, imagine, and create. Scents calm us, such as that from flowers, but so does wet earth, an aroma called "geosmin," according to psychiatrist Sue Stuart-Smith in her book *The Well-Gardened Mind*. She writes: "Green exercise, as it is often called, is more effective at lowering stress levels and improving mood and self-esteem than going to the gym."

Penelope Lively, a British novelist, agrees that gardening is good for us, that we "set spinning our circadian rhythms, jack up our immune systems, and possibly live a few years longer," but in the end, health benefits are irrelevant. "It is simply a matter of intense engagement with cutting back, taking out, putting in, with this rose, that weed, these seeds, bulbs, tubers," she writes in *Life in the Garden*. "As an occupation it seems to me unparalleled; productive, beneficial, enjoyable. What more could you want?"

And so, this spring I will be out in the dirt doing it all again. I will rejoice in the hoeing, weeding, raking, thinning! I will train pea vines, stake tomatoes, hill potatoes, blanch celery, and mulch between rows with the *New York Times* and straw. My seedlings will be transplanted as delicately as I can muster, with all the hope in the world, and I will see what my gardening realm brings this year, dearest delusions of my creative mind.

Sharing a Small Patch of Earth

PUTTING THE VEGETABLE GARDEN TO BED FOR WINTER IS BITTERSWEET. I'M grateful for the garden's abundance, but sad the season is over. With so many chores to accomplish, though, there's little time for contemplation. Trellises have to be taken down, morning glory vines and scarlet runner beans unwound from the white wood. Tomato stakes need to be pulled and the gigantic dahlia bulbs hoisted out of the ground and put in the barn to overwinter in a vat of sawdust. The potato beds—weedy now, the tubers having been dug and some already eaten—are ready for hoeing, in preparation for a cover crop of winter rye. The spent raspberry canes and the wispy asparagus fronds need to be cut back, and the nasturtiums—still bright spots of orange and yellow in an ever-graying world—must be yanked lest they scatter their multitude of seeds, as they so want to do. One can have too many nasturtiums.

I consider picking sorrel to make sorrel soup, a favorite of my mother-in-law—she, long gone now, who taught me so much about gardening. But I will have time for that later, sorrel being the most satisfying of crops, the first to peek out of the soil in my perennial herb bed in spring, and the last to leave. The basil, not so hardy, is withering from cold and turning black, so I pluck some leaves for one last batch of pesto.

My ten-foot sunflower stalks droop sadly, tired of holding up their majestic faces, but I leave the seed heads for the goldfinches, which dart in and out of the tall blooms like dogfighters. My terra-cotta orb is plucked from the meditation circle in the garden's center, and I dig up Jerusalem artichokes to send to a friend in Groton, Massachusetts, who puts them in a delicious tart with chard. Trying to extend the season a tad longer, I drape white row covers over the last planting of lettuce. Gardeners never really give up.

Our two dogs keep me company—a crusty, old golden retriever with a nose any hunter would be proud of, and a goldendoodle puppy who hasn't a clue but follows the other hound enthusiastically. They dig wildly in the dirt, chasing some poor, hapless creature—probably a chipmunk or a vole, or the

rabbit I suspect nibbled at my melons earlier in the season. They rarely catch anything. Something tells me at just the right moment to pick up my weary head and look through the white pickets when I see, scurrying away from me as fast as she can, a brown-furred deer mouse, a new mother with four babies clinging desperately to the teats on her white underbelly and a fifth baby—in her mouth.

The dogs, one anyway, are on her scent and charge enthusiastically in her direction. Normally, I would holler to stop them, but I know they will lose this race, thwarted as they are by having to go around the fence, not through it. Still, watching in what seems like slow motion a mother mouse drag babies on her low-slung belly across thick grass tweaks my maternal DNA, and I think I would do exactly the same—attach my children to my breasts or in my teeth and carry them away from impending danger as quickly as my human feet could muster—exactly as I felt when Flight 93 flew over this garden. I am relieved when the mother mouse darts into the stonewall—the one my husband found solace in building when his mother was ill. The mice find a safe haven—for now at least.

It will be a long, cold winter for those mice, as it will be in our drafty log farmhouse. The mother mouse will huddle with her family as I will with mine. When the days grow longer, I will muse over garden catalogues, contemplating repairs to the raised beds, the plowing and the planting, hopeful for a season better than the last: fewer asparagus beetles, more rain or less, a monster pumpkin, which is all my husband ever wants.

The deer mice, having become torpid in the coldest weather, their body temperatures dropping to 68 degrees, will awaken and have more babies. And since they have three or four litters a year, each with three to seven pups that don't travel far from where they are born, I will encounter them again next spring, burrowing under the straw mulch. We will share this patch of earth together, its family and mine, all of us connected, carving out a brief life on a small western Pennsylvania plot.

Our Sleeping Porch

There was nothing of the giant in the aspect of the man who was beginning to awaken on the sleeping-porch of a Dutch Colonial house in that residential district of Zenith known as Floral Heights. His name was George F. Babbitt.

—From *Babbitt* by Sinclair Lewis

THE JOYS OF A SLEEPING PORCH ARE MANY, BUT THE GREATEST IS A WARM morning before dawn when the windows are flung open, and I lie in bed listening to a chorus of birdsong. As the sun rises, the symphony builds to a crescendo, the notes loud and jumbled, *perhaps* the closest western Pennsylvania will ever get to the sounds of a jungle. I try to distinguish one bird from another, occasionally recognize a Carolina wren or an eastern towhee, but for me the divine pleasure is in the whole.

"Oh, you have a sleeping porch," people always exclaim, their eyes lighting up, when I show them around our old farmhouse. Just before we bought this farm in 1988, my husband and I had slept on a friend's porch in Norfolk, Connecticut, and afterward my husband suggested we add one onto our new bedroom. We enlisted our friend and architect Ellis Schmidlapp and soon found ourselves discussing window treatments, roof angles, and drainage. Ours was the first and only sleeping porch Schmidlapp designed in forty years of architectural practice.

Today, sleeping porches may seem quaint or out of a different time, but they were once standard treatment in domestic architecture, evolving—how odd it feels to write this—during another global health crisis: tuberculosis. TB is an infectious, airborne disease that most commonly affects the lungs and was prevalent in this country from the mid-nineteenth century until the 1940s when streptomycin, an antibiotic, was discovered. TB patients were usually quarantined in sanitoria or at home.

"One of the most important stated goals of the home rest cure was to provide the greatest amount of fresh air possible, to bring the outdoors in,"

94

wrote Katherine Ott in her book *Fevered Lives: Tuberculosis in American Culture since 1870.* Some patients slept outdoors in tents, lean-tos, or cabins; others transformed existing porches into makeshift bedrooms or slept near open windows. The Farlin window tent was a tortuous-looking contraption attached to a window and protruding indoors to cover a patient's upper body. "Around the turn of the century," Ott wrote, "the presence of a sleeping porch indicated respiratory problems in a family as clearly as if a marching band had been hired to announce it." By 1910, "sleeping outdoors and exposure to fresh air had become a part of general middle-class culture."

The Aeroshade Company of Waukesha, Wisconsin, made awnings for sleeping porches in 1916 that "do not absorb and retain heat, but keep it out," and to meet the "popular demand" of sleeping porches, the 1917 Aladdin House Catalog of Bay City, Michigan, which sold house plans, offered two prefabricated sleeping porch additions. "No. 5" was two stories high, ten feet by six feet, the upper story big enough for a double bed, two twins, or three cots, and cost $100, including screens and interior and exterior paint, stain, or oil. The slightly larger "No. 6" was fourteen feet by seven feet and cost $149.50. "The popularity of the sleeping porch needs no comment here," claimed the catalogue copy. "This makes a splendid addition to any house."

Frank Lloyd Wright designed sleeping porches too, including those for western Pennsylvania's own Fallingwater. As Donald Hoffmann wrote in *Frank Lloyd Wright's Fallingwater, The House and its History,* Wright's bedroom designs for Fallingwater were small, simple, and "meant to serve almost as antechambers to their respective terraces, each of which offered more floor space." In 1921, about fourteen years before commissioning Wright to design Fallingwater, the Kaufmanns had built at Bear Run—from the same Aladdin catalogue—a "Readi-cut" cabin with screened porches where, according to Hoffmann, the Kaufmanns had become accustomed to sleeping outside. Then, with the design of Fallingwater underway, Kauffmann had what he called a "bird cage idea" for sleeping on the terraces of his new house. "He discussed it with Wright as early as April 1936," Hoffmann wrote, and Wright made a drawing for a "mobile, steel-framed sleeping chamber." The idea was abandoned, however, in 1937 because a Pittsburgh manufacturer was unable to make the device.

"These ideas were early in the design process," said Justin Gunther, director of Fallingwater, "and whether or not the Kaufmanns ever pulled their walnut-framed beds out onto the terraces at night, I don't know. But it's certainly a romantic notion to think that Liliane might have slept on the master bedroom terrace under the stars!"

The stars and planets are another pleasure of a second-floor sleeping porch such as ours, surrounded as it is on three sides by tall windows and,

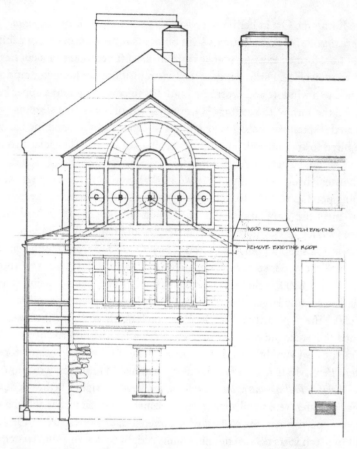

at the gable end, a large fanlight window that allows us to look straight up to the heavens. Schmidlapp said he'd initially pictured conventional double-hung windows for our porch, but my husband wanted windows that swung open into the room and were removable, so we could store them underneath our bed in summertime. The predominantly south-facing room has eleven screened windows in all, and in case they're left open during a rainstorm, Schmidlapp placed drain holes on the floor with a rubber membrane underneath so water wouldn't seep down into the dining room.

Ours is the simplest of interiors: white wainscoting and a gray painted wood floor. I've seen photos of elaborate sleeping porches with wicker furniture, fancy curtains, ceiling fans, shutters, rows of beds with matching bedding, and potted hydrangeas, but we have only a bed, two side tables with lamps for reading, a wooden chest to store warm nightclothes, and a hooked rug. When the children were young, we added a small spindle bed in case they wished to join us. Our dogs always do.

We sleep on our porch year-round, in all weather and all temperatures. I usually draw the line around the freezing mark, but my husband is of stronger stock. Winter takes the most preparation, making sure the windows are shut tightly and piling onto the bed layers of down comforters and sleeping bags. For extra warmth, I've been known to don a red wool "union suit" with a back flap, a nightcap, and socks. Our son remembers when he was young dressing in many layers to sleep out there in winter. "Not for the faint of heart," he said. On the coldest nights, the last thing I do—and my favorite—is to place hot water bottles underneath the sheets before *running* into bed.

On a sleeping porch, the nighttime sounds of wild creatures come close: Great Horned Owls, bullfrogs, fishers, spring peepers, coyotes. We hear the wind howl off the ridge, the roar of a swollen creek below, and rain on the metal roof. Thunder echoes off the walls and lightning illuminates the room. Some nights, we watch the full arc of the moon rise and set, and on moonless nights, identify constellations. Winter brings the first scent of snow and in summer, fireflies sparkle around us. When a chill takes hold in autumn, the sleeping porch retains the sun's warmth and becomes a solarium of sorts—a wonderful place to meditate, read a book, or nap.

But who wants to *sleep* on a sleeping porch when the world offers such gifts?

THE
ENVIRONMENT

Less Lawn, More Native Plants

WHEN MY MOTHER-IN-LAW WAS ILL TWENTY-EIGHT YEARS AGO, MY HUS-band began to build a stone wall on our front lawn. Each rock he handled three, maybe four times: plucked from the woods, thrown into the back of a pick-up, dropped onto the grass to decide placement, or set directly atop a dry wall. One stone at a time, he dealt with his grief. Hour after hour, I saw him grimace under the weight of the boulders. I heard him groan. I wondered what were his thoughts, but I needn't have asked him, and he needn't have told me. Ten feet, then fifty, and finally four hundred feet long, the wall, I knew, was dedicated, silently, to his mother.

He left spaces in the wall for two wooden gates so we could walk to the pond, the hammock, or into the woods. Outside those gates he's always mown the grass, but last summer, for the first time, he did not. The grasses grew tall, golden brown, and swayed in the wind. The only mown sections were three long, meandering paths—emerald green and beckoning me uphill toward the forest beyond. The vista was looser and more relaxed, the way I realized I'd always envisioned it.

Inspired by entomologist Douglas Tallamy's book *Nature's Best Hope*, we reduced the size of our front lawn by more than half. Forty million acres of lawn exist in this country, the size of New England, with five hundred square miles added each year, what Tallamy called "ecological dead space." Since 86 percent of the land east of the Mississippi is privately owned, homeowners, he believes, must preserve land "where we live, work, and farm." In 2020, Tallamy started Homegrown National Park, an organization that encourages people to reduce lawn, plant more native plants, remove invasive plants, and add their names to an online map. As of this writing, 924 people have signed up in Pennsylvania and 23 here in Westmoreland County.

Tallamy doesn't say we need to get rid of all our lawn. He understands lawn is nice to walk on in bare feet and that it's a status symbol in this country, but by shrinking our lawns and growing native plants, he said, we sustain food webs, store carbon, manage watersheds, rebuild soils, and support

pollinators. If all of us do this, whether a
few acres or a 3' x 7' patch, we create
wildlife corridors for insects, birds,
and other creatures as they move
around, migrate, and reproduce.

Many of us have known for a
while now about the importance of
native plants and the decline of honeybees and monarch butterflies, but
this farm has many wild areas, so I
think perhaps I'd given myself an
ecological free pass. Then I made a
list of all the ornamental plants in
my flower garden, and I was embar-
rassed. Welcome to my Asian garden, with
a good dose of influence from Gertrud
Jekyll and the English cottage garden:
peonies, hydrangea, Japanese anem-
one, delphinium, hollyhock, and more.
Granted we have fields and forests of goldenrod, aster, spicebush, Joe-Pye weed, and other
native plants crucial for our western Pennsylvania ecosystem, but I don't get a free pass; we must all do our part.

I called Douglas Tallamy and was grateful he wasn't as critical of me as I
was of myself. "There's room for compromise," he said. "You don't need to be
100 percent native." Just increase the number of native plants in my yard, he
said, and I'd be "doing a good thing." Most people grow gardens for aesthetics,
and he doesn't want people to lose the entertainment value of gardens, but a
large percentage of plants from Asia is not a good ratio.

In this country, 3,300 invasive plant species exist, and 85 percent of the
invasive woody plants come from our gardens. These crowd out our native
plants, which are important because they support our native insects—and
native insects, according to Tallamy, "are fussy about what they eat." It's not
just the connection between milkweed and the monarch butterfly; nettle
is the host plant for the red admiral butterfly and aster for the pearl cres-
cent butterfly. Hackberry supports the hackberry emperor butterfly. The
double-toothed prominent moth can't live without our native elms. "The
most important and abundant specialized relationships on the planet are
the relationships among the insects that eat plants and the plants they
eat," Tallamy said.

Biologist E.O. Wilson called insects "the little things that run the world," and they are in peril, their numbers down 45 percent worldwide since 1975. Bats and hummingbirds pollinate, but it's mostly bees, Tallamy said, which pollinate 90 percent of all flowering plants. And while we've been rallying around the non-native honeybee, we have four thousand species of native bees to protect. Three North American bumblebees are extinct already, with 25 percent at risk of extinction; so are 30 percent of grasshoppers, crickets, and katydids. "By killing insects, we are biting the hand that feeds us," Tallamy said.

But what about the bees I see sipping enthusiastically on some of my non-native plants, such as borage, poppies, and catmint? Tallamy explained that while such non-natives do produce nectar, they may not make the pollen that supports our specialist bees. "It takes enormous periods of time before introduced plants act like the natives they replace," Tallamy said; what he called "a glacial rate of evolutionary change."

Replacing non-native plants with natives—also called straight species—can be confusing, however. The first step at least was easy: finding plants native to western Pennsylvania, and I did so by typing my zip code into two websites: nwf.org/NativePlantFinder and audubon.org/native-plants. I was pleased that I already grow some of the recommended plants, such as monarda, baptisia, and phlox, but the problem is that my plants could be cultivars and, depending on how the plant is altered, might not serve our native insects as well.

Knowing the Latin name of a plant is key here, although I laugh at myself as I write this. My dear, departed mother-in-law—a great gardener—urged me early on to learn a plant's Latin name, and I scoffed, finding such advice rather highfalutin for a beginning gardener. But like many things our elders teach us, she was correct. Take, for example, loosestrife. *Lythrum salicaria* is a non-native that threatens wetlands, and *Lythrum alatum* is native and "of special value to native bees," according to the Xerxes Society for Invertebrate Conservation.

Where then do I find the natives? Websites exist, but since I buy most of my plants locally, I wondered if my nursery or farmer's market carry them. In an effort to garden environmentally in the past, I've asked big-box garden store employees whether plants contain neonicotinoids and my local farm store about purchasing peat-free compost, and both times I've received blank stares in return. Still, Tallamy advised me to persevere. "Ask for the straight species," he said. "If we send the message that there's a market for straight species, more people will carry them."

One local nursery, Friendship Farms in Latrobe, does specialize in native plants. Joe Costello and his brother, Mike, decided twenty years ago to sell

what the big nurseries did not. "We wanted to do something different," he said. "We didn't know it would become a 'thing.'" The nursery specializes in large habitat plantings for such clients as the Pennsylvania Game Commission, but sells to individuals as well. He warned, however, that some homeowners don't like the straggly look of native plants—they look better in the wild than against the house. "It takes some getting used to," he said. "Start small and work your way up from there."

No Mow May was begun in the UK as a citizen's science project and adopted in 2020 by Appleton, Wisconsin, when the city council suspended their weed ordinance for the month of May. This organization urges people not to mow grass in May, which creates habitat and forage for early season pollinators. In our old cow field, No Mow May turned into No Mow June and then No Mow Summer, and the field bloomed into a glorious color combination of white, purple, yellow, and tan: grasses mixed with non-native Queen Anne's lace and natives ironweed, goldenrod, and brown-eyed Susan, good for bees and butterflies.

Nature's Best Hope changed the way I look at the flora and fauna on this farm and I love that I can make change right here and now to help the environment. This winter, I'm making a list of what else I can do. One is to locate invasive species, such as Japanese barberry, multiflora rose, privet, and burning bush, though removal would be no easy feat. I planted none of it, but such plants have naturalized all over this farm. Another is to resist eradicating what we call "weeds," especially goldenrod, which support many caterpillar species. Until I read Tallamy's book, I had no idea the importance of caterpillars to our ecosystem, particularly to bird populations. Chickadees, for instance, feed their babies six thousand to nine thousand caterpillars for the two weeks they are in the nest. That's one brood, in one year, by one bird species. "Caterpillars are the most important accessible currency to measure the food web," Tallamy said. We need caterpillars!

I will rethink fall cleanup chores, including raking leaves, because caterpillars pupate in fallen leaves, and I'll try to be less tidy and leave the seed heads on such plants as rudbeckia, good winter forage for bees. "The social edict to neaten up is often in direct conflict with the needs of our native bees," Tallamy said.

Perhaps most important, however, is to plant more trees and shrubs, particularly what Tallamy called keystone plants—those that have the largest effect on the abundance and diversity of species in an ecosystem. "Without keystone plants," he said, "the food web all but falls apart." The best tree to plant is the white oak, my husband's favorite, which he's planted and nurtured over many years. "Oaks support more life forms than any other North American tree genus," Tallamy said, "including over 950 species of the caterpillars that support breeding birds."

My husband will plant more oaks on the farm. I'll plant keystone shrubs and flowers. Together we'll work to make the farm a better place for all the creatures living among us—and for the humans renting the space.

One stone—or plant—at a time.

Litter

Last year, I rode my bike on back roads near our farm. I prefer swimming, but our YMCA was closed, so I dusted off my thirty-year-old red Cannondale and set out in a beautiful valley between two ridges of the Allegheny mountains. My favorite ride was a seven-mile loop with eleven steep hills, up which I pedaled slowly, and as I did, I saw something on the road I'd never noticed from a car: huge amounts of litter.

I've always disliked litter, perhaps because I heeded the anti-litter slogans of my childhood: Don't be a Litterbug and Every Litter Bit Hurts. Even at a young age, I believed such slogans were created for the good of the planet, and I wanted to contribute to that cause. But I was naïve. According to Heather Roger's book *Gone Tomorrow, The Hidden Life of Garbage*, those anti-litter campaigns were dreamed up in the middle of the last century by American Can, the Owens-Illinois Glass Company, Dixie Cup, Coca-Cola, and other companies to prevent them from having to manufacture more expensive, refillable containers—and the campaigns were promoted by a newly formed organization called Keep America Beautiful. "The centerpiece of the organization's strategy was its great cultural invention: '*litter*,'" Rogers writes, and the real villain was not the bottle and can companies, but "the notorious litterbug."

I may have been well indoctrinated, but nevertheless I still don't want to be a litterbug. I've never understood people who roll down car windows and toss out soda cans, and as I biked past filthy beer bottles and rusty power drink cans, I got madder with each bike ride—rides that were supposed to calm my mind during a global pandemic. So, one hot and humid day, still in my biking clothes, with an arthritic right ankle that falters on uneven surfaces, I got into the car and ventured out to pick up the litter along my bike route.

My first stop was Horseshoe Bend, a dangerous state road with a hairpin turn and numerous blind spots. I put on my flashers—or four-ways as they call them here in Appalachia—parked on the berm when I could, and raised my car's trunk to be more obvious. I attempted to wear gloves, but I'd grabbed my husband's extra-large, ill-fitting canvas work gloves, with which I could hardly grasp the garbage, so I often used my bare hands, not the wisest move during Covid-19. I tiptoed over poison ivy; cut my shin, which bled; and spilled beer and 7-Up on my bare legs. My ankle hurt climbing up and down ravines, I encountered a foul smelling, fly-ridden opossum, and ants got inside the car and crawled on me. I worried about ticks. At least I had the pleasure of the song of the wood thrush as I walked.

One stretch of Horseshoe Bend borders our woods, woods filled with chanterelles, scarlet cup mushrooms, and wild blackberries, but there was none of that beauty on the adjacent roadside—only brown shrubs, dead thistle, and a few sprigs of Queen Anne's lace. That's because Pennsylvania mows and sprays its state roads with any one of numerous herbicides: Round-Up, Escort, Arsenal, Vastlan, Polaris, Pathfinder II, Vanquish, Krenite-S, Assure II, and Rodeo, according to Jan Huzvar, deputy communications director of the Pennsylvania Department of Transportation (PennDot). And I was traipsing through it all.

What a pile of junk I collected: ten plastic water bottles, one Coke, four Pepsi, six energy drinks, one Bootlegger raspberry liquor, twenty-five beer cans—Coors, Budweiser, and Keystone Light (and the plastic bag they came in)—six supersized cups (McDonald's, Dairy Queen, and Wendy's), a Wonder Bread bag, one reflector, two lottery tickets, tire shreds, a straw, french-fry boxes, a chia squeeze drink, a plastic salad container, a pair of protective glasses, weed whacking string, a car fender, a Chicken McNuggets wrapper, a cardboard Coors Light carrier, two aluminum pipes, torn food wrappers, and a large a red Dixie cup.

Some items I left on purpose, such as plastic flowers that blew out of a cemetery, which I felt deserved respect, concrete slabs I couldn't lift, and a dirty diaper I wasn't able to reach down a steep hill. And I know I missed a green chewing tobacco canister I'd seen on a bike ride, so it's still out there—somewhere. At my last two stops, I found a bag of used insulin needles and a water bottle filled with more needles.

My litter sample was small, however, compared to what the *Pennsylvania Litter Research Study* estimates clogs our roadways on any given day: 502.5 million pieces of litter, including 186.2 million cigarette butts; 152.9 million pieces of plastic; 61,546,655 pieces of paper; 32,182,246 pieces of metal; 29.3 million beverage containers; 12.3 million fast food items; and 5,628,179 pieces of glass. Rural roads, such as Horseshoe Bend, are estimated to have 1,635 litter items per mile.

"Pennsylvania has a littering habit" opened a press release announcing the study, released in November 2019 at a "Litter Summit" in Harrisburg. Funded by PennDot, Pennsylvania's Department of Environmental Protection (DEP), and Keep Pennsylvania Beautiful (a state affiliate of Keep America Beautiful), the study monitored litter in one hundred eighty Pennsylvania sites, including nine cities, and the resulting one-hundred-ten-page report concluded that "reducing littering behavior is key to a clean, beautiful, healthier, and more prosperous Pennsylvania."

I returned home, sweaty and tired, to a husband angry that I'd used my bare hands to fetch someone's needles. I showered with pink antibacterial soap prescribed to him before a surgery, then called Farley Toothman, a friend who was a judge in a neighboring county and asked him if he'd ever tried anyone for littering. Not in ten years on the bench, he said. "It's horrific, but it's not enforced anywhere." He told me those needles were not used for insulin, but likely for heroin or other drugs.

Now I had another problem: How was I to dispose of medical waste? I called our borough office, but no one answered. The police department didn't call back. The police chief didn't answer my email. The township supervisor's office didn't know, but said local citizens, not the state, clean our roads, including the Girl and Boy Scouts, but Horseshoe Bend is too dangerous for children. If I wanted to know more, she advised me not to call PennDot because they don't call back, but instead to file a complaint on their website. I did so, filled out the required form, and laughed at its closing line: *Are you sure you want to submit this concern?"*

Hell yes.

Twenty-four hours later, a PennDot representative left me a message concerning my "customer care concern." Whoever had cleaned up litter on Horseshoe Bend had quit, he said, so the road was now available for an "Adopt-A-Highway" slot. I called back for details, but he didn't return my call. I logged on to the Adopt-A-Highway website, which flashed so violently my cursor barely worked, but I could read enough to learn that in order to adopt a highway, applicants must be eight years old and include someone eighteen or older. Adoption requires cleaning a highway for two years and allows the construction of roadside memorials. For litter cleanup, PennDot will supply vests, trash bags, and "Litter Crew Ahead" signs.

But Susan Huba, executive director of The Loyalhanna Watershed Association, a local environmental group that organizes litter cleanup, said getting donated supplies from PennDot is difficult. "They fight us every year with the amount of material we need," she said. If she asks for five hundred garbage bags, they supply four hundred. "I feel like I have to sell my first-born child to get enough bags."

The state doesn't clean up, she said, only picks up trash bags that her crews leave at designated spots, and "it takes them weeks to do so." Animals often get into the bags and spread garbage everywhere. During one cleanup, she asked to close one lane of a narrow road where people drive fast but was turned down. She's been yelled at twice by police who said she shouldn't be out there at all, but if she must, "You should do this at 5:00 a.m. on a Sunday." She told me a story about the state mowing grass near the organization's property and instead of removing a mattress someone had tossed, they mowed over it.

But Deborah Klenotic, deputy communications director of DEP, disagreed that the state does nothing about litter. "Without PennDot and DEP funding and supplies," she said, "litter collection wouldn't exist." Klenotic said the study revealed to her that Pennsylvania needs to shift its emphasis from cleanup to prevention. "Cleanup is astronomically expensive and we can't keep pace with the littering that's happening," she said. The nine cities studied spend $68.5 million annually on litter cleanup, and PennDot spends $13 million.

Litterbugs simply assume someone else will clean up after them, said Shannon Reiter, KPB's executive director. "We have to have a certain level of pride in ourselves," she said. "Why are we trashing our communities?"

Litter may not be the most talked about environmental issue, but it's something we confront every day where we live and work, and, according to the study, has a host of repercussions: raises taxes, reduces property values, negatively impacts business and tourism, injures children, stunts plant growth, kills wildlife, and may cause more crime and vehicle accidents. The study outlined a plan to educate residents, increase trash cans, develop

partnerships, assist communities, and study litter ordinances, laws, statutes, and enforcement.

But David Masur, executive director of PennEnvironment, a state environmental group, doesn't believe education, cleanup, or enforcement are the answers. "For fifty years, we've tried the litterbug thing and the Native American riding his horse with the tear drop in his eye. That stuff only got us so far." The key, he said, is fewer or no plastic bags and a bottle deposit. "We have to reduce front-end consumption," he said. "The manufacturers are basically saying it's your problem. You figure it out. The tail-end fixing of the problem is not a viable solution."

My solution was to adopt Horseshoe Bend, so I tracked down another PennDot employee. She kindly filled out a form for me (my cursor still wouldn't work on their website) and instructed me to sign an agreement and watch safety videos, which I did. In the meantime, PennDot would study Horseshoe Bend's traffic volume, road shoulders, and crash data. While I waited for approval, I made a plan. I'll go out on a less hot day, wear an orange vest, long pants, hiking boots, and properly fitting gloves. I'll request trash bags and official signage, gather together a group of like-minded friends, and we will clean up our stretch of Pennsylvania's country roads.

But a couple of weeks later, I was told that my request had been denied; Horseshoe Bend was too dangerous. Who will clean our road then, I asked? She didn't know.

I have biked many times since, and the litter is back, but now there are soy sauce packets, eggshells, milk cartons, athletic socks—and masks.

And what about those needles I found? For weeks they sat in a coffee can on a shelf in the barn. It took two more phone calls, to our county recycling expert, to get an answer. She instructed me to put the needles in a detergent bottle, tape the lid, write POISON or draw a skull and crossbones on top, and toss them into my household trash.

Marcellus Shale Seismic Testing

One beautiful Friday in November, I was working in my vegetable garden when I saw a helicopter fly low over our house. Attached to it was a long wire carrying multiple orange sacks. The helicopter lowered just beyond the pond and dropped some of the sacks. About a half-hour later it flew over again, repeating the procedure.

The next day, I went into the woods looking for the sacks and located two. I met a fellow who said he worked for Geokinetics, a seismic testing company involved in the extraction of shale gas. Armed with a GPS device, he was trying to locate all of the testing materials, which, he said, comprised two stations of dynamite and twenty-three recording devices.

This was just over our property line, on the property of a neighbor, who had permitted the blasting. My concern was that if the testing company was inexact, explosions might be near the trails where we ride horses and walk or near our spring, from which we drink.

The man explained that he was an employee and didn't know what was going on. I asked him for a business card, but he didn't have one. He offered to have his boss call me, and within an hour, a fellow from McDonald Land Services did so, explaining that he was hired by Williams, a Marcellus Shale gas drilling company, to conduct seismic testing on the property next to ours. I asked if he would kindly tell me when the dynamite would be detonated so that we could take precautions. With a lovely Arkansas accent, he agreed to do so.

Then I wondered: Why am I asking someone from a faraway state to notify me when he is about to set off explosives near my house? Shouldn't I have been offered information or help from my federal, state, or local governments?

I turned to the Penn State Marcellus Shale Center for Outreach and Research, which advises landowners to be vigilant about protecting their water supply during seismic testing.

Fine, but where does that leave those of us who live in rural communities as we face a massive, confusing invasion of industrial operations? We are left to our own devices to protect ourselves, our land, our water, our air, our animals, and our children.

A friend, trying to do just that, found orange seismic flags on the road next to her barn and demanded an explanation from Williams. Suddenly, with three days' notice, an informational session was called in Cook Township in Westmoreland County.

I went and asked the McDonald Land Services representative if his company planned to notify people who might be affected by seismic testing on a neighbor's property. I inferred from what he said that his company had no legal obligation to do so, but he said he wanted "to make communication with everyone." He had confidence that his men were on the correct property and gave high praise to the Westmoreland office of Geographic Information Services. "These guys are good. If you see them, tell them they are great," he said.

The following day at dusk, my husband and I saw two men in orange jackets sitting on a stone wall in our backyard. A third man stood next to them. From a distance, I figured they were hunters, as it was the first day of bear season and men with high-powered rifles were everywhere.

We asked what they were up to, but they claimed not to speak English. Within ten minutes, two more men came out of our woods carrying armloads of canisters and wires, which they dropped on our lawn. Only one of them spoke a modicum of English. He produced a business card: Cougar Land

Services, based in Stafford, Texas, but with a Bakersfield, California, phone number and a cell number with a 330 area code.

We asked them to leave and I followed them to the access road from which they came. A white truck with the name GreyCo on the side overflowed with workers. (This would be GreyCo Seismic Personnel Services of Houston, Texas.)

By my count, that's five companies, which I presume subcontract to each other. Is it a coincidence that one of them hires workers, some of whom don't speak our language and cannot explain what they are doing on our property? And what about the local jobs that gas drilling is supposed to create?

The GreyCo driver, who did speak English, pulled out a map and said he had every right to be on our property. He pointed out where he thought his men were, but he clearly had no idea. He said it was not his fault.

The next day, a Sunday, my husband and I heard blasts, with no prior warning from the Arkansas gentleman. Helicopters circled overhead. I had just come in from horseback riding with my husband and our ten-year-old neighbor. (Bear season is suspended on Sundays, but apparently not seismic testing.)

I am well aware that Marcellus Shale gas is a huge, burgeoning industry that can provide energy for millions of people in our country, and that many in our rural community will make large sums of money. I know gas drilling is here to stay and that I could next be faced with a worse fate than seismic testing: a gigantic drilling rig right next door.

But in Cook Township we are in the beginning stages of dealing with this industry, and if this is how these companies—the same ones that want to lease my gas rights—act with dynamite, why would I expect anything better from them when dealing with earthmoving equipment, drilling rigs, fracking fluid, holding ponds, or pipelines?

In America, industry has the freedom to develop opportunities and make money. But as a citizen face-to-face with behemoth industrial might, I expect better protection from my government. How is it that pretty soon I will only be able to buy one kind of light bulb while big national gas companies can operate at will in my backyard? It is high time we change that.

Quarantine on the Farm

FARM ANIMALS KNOW NO QUARANTINE. HORSES MUST BE FED AND BROUGHT in from pasture, stalls mucked out, winter coats clipped. The farrier arrives.

I pluck chicken eggs warm from nesting boxes. I try to order female peeps from my usual supplier, but they are sold out, so I put a Buff Cochin rooster with four hens to hatch my own.

Our fields need to be mowed, trails cleared, firewood cut. My husband manages this, wanders deep into the forest, lugging the chain saw and pole pruner, his meditation on the world. He loves trees—plants them, prunes them, stakes them, pulls wild grape off branches to prevent suffocation.

We begin sheltering at home in winter, cold and gray. Snow falls. Wind howls off the mountain. A tornado touches down near our farm.

I wait for the children to come home, my wings outstretched, ready to shield them from an invisible pathogen. But they do not come. Our son works in Argentina, our daughter in Boston. On 9/11, I felt similarly—get home fast, huddle together, stay there—even though Flight 93 went over this farm, over the children's school. It takes a global pandemic for me to admit they won't be home long-term again, and I'm sad, until a friend reminds me: We raised our children to have strong wings. And so they do.

Quarantine allows me to slow down and, leaving the farm now as little as possible, to look even more closely at the natural world. At first, nature appears to carry on. Ice covers the pond's perimeter, and then globules of gelatinous eggs appear at the water's edge. Wood frogs and spotted salamanders will be born. Canada geese land, and a breeding pair of mallards. The great blue heron and kingfisher will circle back, and soon tiny heads of snapping turtles will rise from the muddy depths and break the water's surface. I count the days until I can swim again. I have dunked every month except February, but I miss the long stretch and pull of a good lap.

Spring comes anyway, virus or no. Yellow is the earliest color: forsythia, dandelions, daffodils. On Easter morning, I listen to hymns by the fire, then witness rebirth in the vegetable garden: sorrel, lemon balm, lovage.

Chickweed, slowed by no plague, covers the asparagus and strawberry beds. That will take some strong weeding, I think, until I consider: If food gets rationed, I can make chickweed pesto.

My vegetable garden, which I've planted every year for thirty years, is a victory garden now. I aim to be even more self-sufficient, and there is work to do: soil turned over, raised beds repaired, compost added, paths mulched. I tiptoe through mud, plant chervil, turnips, and snap peas. I cut spent raspberry canes. The garlic I planted last fall, before I had an inkling of how the world was about to turn, shows life. And the parrot tulips emerge, frilled and gaudy, my own quarantine tulip mania.

While gardening, I think of my older brother. He has Covid-19. His family shelters together; all five may have the disease. His daughter's case is mild, but my brother needs to catch his breath at the top of the stairs, can barely walk from shower to bed, says he feels as he did when going through chemotherapy. He feels better, then much worse. He is so tired he asks his wife to handle communication.

No pandemic stops the feral honeybees. A hive has wintered in a hole in a walnut tree, just below the hole where a rat snake lives. Hundreds of bees sip wildly from the orange-red blossoms of the quince. I stand underneath the branches, just to listen.

My younger brother calls. He is out of work.

A woodchuck (perhaps) living under an outbuilding still makes its way to the bird feeder every night. I can see its path. The black bear will probably rip out the wooden rungs on that feeder, as it did last year. White-tailed deer sneak in close to the house, nibbling on euonymus. Chipmunks scamper about, eating my crocus bulbs. Wild turkeys cross the grass, and a fox, probably with kits to feed, watches me one evening as I shut the chicken coop. Coyotes will howl and the fisher will scream—creatures circling us, the wolves at the door of our human health.

A high school friend goes to the hospital with Covid-19 but is sent home. She worsens. Her oxygen levels are low, so her husband takes her back. When she's admitted, there are six Covid-19 patients. When she leaves two weeks later, ninety. The fourth drug administered, an HIV drug, pulls her through.

The birds return, singing: red-winged blackbirds, rose-breasted grosbeak, the eastern towhee. At dawn from our sleeping porch, their chorus lifts my spirit. I follow a scarlet tanager that hops on rocks in the stream. That behavior isn't normal, but the color astonishes me, as does the blue of an indigo bunting, the orange of an oriole, the yellow of a goldfinch. Barn swallows nest again in the garage, a soft rain of nest-making materials falling on my car.

My brother improves, but then gets pleurisy.

Nature takes a strange turn. The bees swarm three times, and I must get closer than six feet to coax them into an old bee box. I see a migrating coot, the first in thirty-one years. A rabid raccoon greets me midmorning in the vegetable garden, digs in the dirt, then tumbles off a raised bed and drags its hind-end back through the pickets. Two hawks attack a flicker near an apple tree. I get gloves and pick it up, never having seen a flicker so close and marveling at its red neck ring and bright yellow wing stripes. I try to save it, but it dies.

Mother's Day weekend brings snow and record low temperatures. The freeze takes the glory out of the magnolia and wisteria, even the hostas—a plant I thought could survive nuclear winter. I notice strange behavior in another scarlet tanager, and after two dead birds are taken to the local nature reserve, the director blames hypothermia.

I know I am fortunate to be on this farm, to be healthy and have room to move around, but the dying flora and fauna and the horrible human toll of Covid-19 rattle me, and I worry for my children, our country, the world. Usually, I find solace in the woods, so I take long walks, forage for morels and ramps, pick watercress by the stream. But this time, I hear our planet pleading, far away at first—bird populations plummeting, insects dying, arctic ice melting, the Amazon burning—and then closer to home.

Nature is not just carrying on. Chimney swifts, which roost every summer in our nineteenth-century chimney, have declined by 72 percent. The emerald ash borer has killed hundreds of our ash trees. Our summers are hotter and wetter. The "100-year flood" has come about five times in the last twelve years. Nearby, water is contaminated by fracking. Nary a bat can be seen in the night sky, lost to white-nose syndrome. My maple sugaring friends can't decide when to tap trees because of climate change.

In my small slice of the world, I see a neon sign flashing red, and I wonder how long can we go on without seeing and without listening—to the bats, the bugs, the bees, the birds, the trees, the land?

My hope is that when the pandemic releases its grip, when the world speeds up again and we return to work and school, when there's less time to watch birds and weed a victory garden, that we remember what Covid-19 has taught us: that our health and our planet's health have never been more intertwined—and to take care of the planet is to take care of ourselves.

As quarantine lifts and spring turns toward summer, one of our hens finally broods. Fourteen eggs beneath her, she stays on the nest hour after hour, eating and drinking only occasionally, a long twenty-one days. Each time I visit, she looks more bedraggled, as if she is wasting away. She used to get up when I brought kitchen scraps, but now she won't leave her clutch even for lettuce. Every day she sits, warming the life beneath her, full of hope.

BIBLIOGRAPHY

Andrews, Ted. *Animal Speak: The Spiritual and Magical Powers of Creatures Great & Small*. Woodbury, MN: Llewellyn Publications, 2002.

Beresford-Kroeger, Diana. *To Speak for the Trees: My Life's Journey from Ancient Celtic Wisdom to a Healing Vision of the Forest*. Toronto: Random House Canada, 2019.

Boyd, William K. and Percy G. Adams. *William Byrd's Histories of the Dividing Line betwixt Virginia and North Carolina*. Mineola, NY: Dover Publications, 1967.

Damerow, Gail. *Storey's Guide to Raising Chickens, 4th Edition*. North Adams, MA: Storey Publishing, 2017.

Day, Mary F. "Home Life in a Chimney." *Bird Lore Magazine*, 1899.

Faust, Lynn Frierson. *Fireflies, Glow-worms, and Lightning Bugs: Identification and Natural History of the Fireflies of the Eastern and Central United States and Canada*. Athens, GA: University of Georgia Press, 2017.

Gibbons, Euell. *Stalking the Wild Asparagus*. Guilford, CT: Stackpole Books, 2020.

Goldfarb, Ben. *Eager: The Surprising, Secret Life of Beavers and Why They Matter*. White River Junction, VT: Chelsea Green Publishing, 2018.

Hoffmann, Donald. *Frank Lloyd Wright's Fallingwater: The House and Its History*. Mineola, NY: Dover Publications, 1993.

Kimmerer, Robin Wall. *Gathering Moss: A Natural and Cultural History of Mosses*. Corvallis, OR: Oregon State University Press, 2003.

Klips, Robert. *Common Mosses, Liverworts, and Lichens of Ohio: A Visual Guide*. Athens, OH: Ohio University Press, 2022.

Kuo, Michael. *Morels*. Ann Arbor, MI: University of Michigan Regional, 2005.

Kyle, Paul, and Georgean Kyle. *Chimney Swifts: America's Mysterious Birds Above the Fireplace*. College Station, TX: Texas A&M University Press, 2005.

Lincoff, Gary. *The Complete Mushroom Hunter, Revised*. Beverly, MA: Quarry Books, 2017.

Lively, Penelope. *Life in the Garden*. New York: Viking, 2018.

Loohuizen, Ria. *The Elder: In History, Myth and Cookery*. London: Prospect Books, 2004.

Mercia, Leonard S. *Raising Poultry the Modern Way*. Pownal, VT: Storey Communications, Inc., 1975.

Ott, Katherine. *Fevered Lives: Tuberculosis in American Culture since 1870*. Cambridge, MA: Harvard University Press, 1999.

Rezendes, Paul. *Tracking & the Art of Seeing: How to Read Animal Tracks & Sign*. Columbia, SC: Camden House, 1992.

Rogers, Heather. *Gone Tomorrow: The Hidden Life of Garbage*. New York: The New Press, 2006.

Roze, Uldis. *The North American Porcupine, 2nd Edition*. Ithaca, NY: Comstock Publishing Associates, 2009.

Seeley, Thomas D. *Honeybee Democracy*. Princeton, NJ: Princeton University Press, 2010.

Sherman, Althea R. *Birds of an Iowa Dooryard*. Iowa City, IA: University of Iowa Press, 1996.

Sibley, David Allen. *What It's Like to be a Bird: From Flying to Nesting, Eating to Singing—What Birds Are Doing, and Why*. New York: Knopf, 2020.

Spielman, Linda J. *A Field Guide to Tracking Mammals in the Northeast*. Woodstock, VT: Countryman Press, 2017.

Stuart-Smith, Sue. *The Well Gardened Mind: Rediscovering Nature in the Modern World*. New York: Scribner, 2020.

Tallamy, Douglas W. *Nature's Best Hope*. Portland, OR: Timber Press, 2019.

Taylor, David A. *Ginseng, the Divine Root: The Curious History of the Plant That Captivated the World*. Chapel Hill, NC: Algonquin, 2006.

Wagner, David L. *Caterpillars of Eastern North America*. Princeton, NJ: Princeton University Press, 2005.

White, E. B. *Charlotte's Web*. New York: Harper & Brothers, 1952.

Whittemore, Margaret. *Chimney Swifts and their Relatives*. Jackson, MS: Nature Books Publishers, 1981.

Wigginton, Eliot. *Foxfire 3: Animal Care, Banjos and Dulcimers, Hide Tanning, Summer and Fall Wild Plant Foods, Butter Churns, Ginseng, and Still More Affairs of Plain Living*. New York: Anchor Books, 1975.

Wohlleben, Peter. *The Hidden Life of Trees: What They Feel, How They Communicate—Discoveries from a Secret World*. Vancouver: Greystone Books, 2016.

About the Author

Daryln Brewer Hoffstot is a freelance writer whose work has appeared in numerous publications, including the *New York Times*, the *Boston Globe*, and *Pittsburgh Quarterly*. Her essay in the *New York Times*, "On a Pennsylvania Farm, Nature Is Not Just Carrying On," won a Notable Mention in *The Best American Science and Nature Writing 2021*. She lives in Ligonier, Pennsylvania.

9 780811 772457